SELF-EVIDENCE

Pamela White Hadas

S ELF - EVIDENCE

A Selection of Verse
1977–1997

TRIQUARTERLY BOOKS
NORTHWESTERN UNIVERSITY PRESS
EVANSTON, ILLINOIS

TriQuarterly Books
Northwestern University Press
Evanston, Illinois 60208-4210

Printed in the United States of America

ISBN 0-8101-5073-5 (cloth)
ISBN 0-8101-5074-3 (paper)

Library of Congress Cataloging-in-Publication Data

Hadas, Pamela White.
        Self evidence : a selection of verse, 1977–1997 / Pamela White Hadas.
        p. cm.
        ISBN 0-8101-5073-5 (alk. paper). — ISBN 0-8101-5074-3 (pbk. : alk. paper)
        1. Women—Poetry. I. Title.
PS3558.A311598S45 1998
811'.54—dc21   97-47361
                                                                         CIP

The paper used in this publication meets the minimum requirements of the Amer-
ican National Standard for Information Sciences—Permanence of Paper for Printed
Library Materials, ANSI z39.48-1984.

*For my mother, with love, and in loving memory of my brother,
James Gregory White (1948–1994)*

He thought he kept the universe alone;
For all the voice in answer he could wake
Was but the mocking echo of his own
From some tree-hidden cliff across the lake.
Some morning from the boulder-broken beach
He would cry out on life, that what it wants
Is not its own love back in copy speech,
But counter-love, original response.

— Robert Frost, "The Most of It"

CONTENTS

$\mathcal{A}$CKNOWLEDGMENTS

Many of the poems included in this volume originally appeared in the following collections: *Designing Women* (Knopf, 1979); *In Light of Genesis* (Jewish Publication Society, 1981); and *Beside Herself: Pocahontas to Patty Hearst* (Knopf, 1983). "'Jung and Easily Freudened'" originally appeared in *The Columbia Review.* "Queen Charming Writes Again" and "Woman with Gardenia" appeared in quite different versions in *The Bread Loaf Anthology of Poetry* (1985). Parts of "From the Opus of Wilhelmina Scrowd" first appeared in *Missouri Women Writers* (1987). The poems are not in their original or chronological order; each section of this book contains early as well as recent work.

I would like to thank Conrad Bishop and Elizabeth Fuller of The Independent Eye Theater in Philadelphia for their splendid production of *Beside Herself.* I have learned from the visions, insights, and energy of their performances; I smile whenever I think of Elizabeth transforming herself from a teenage Pocahontas into Martha Mitchell mad about Watergate. I thank Jane Alpert from the bottom of my heart for her years of patient help in revising and understanding and believing in my work. I thank my editors at Northwestern, Reginald Gibbons and Ellen Feldman. Every suggestion and query of theirs helps my work look a little smarter than I am. I am especially grateful to Reg for listening through the silence and bringing me out of it.

Part One   *S* H O W   &   T E L L

Art is design, Love.
    Thus do I draw the fine
Thin bones of
    Your hand into mine.

— P. Hecate

$\mathcal{S}$ARAH: DEPARTURES, VOICES

for Sarah Hadas

> *Abraham I can't understand,*
> *in a certain sense there is nothing I can learn from him*
> *but astonishment.*
>
> — Kierkegaard, *Fear and Trembling*

The First Departure: marrying Abram

I knew before I married him.
He wasn't such a good catch as my mother said.
I'd seen this uncle of mine in the market
hawking wooden models of Nimrod's gods.
I saw him laugh in an old woman's face
because she wanted to buy something precious.

Idols. A respected old family business.
But toy gods never suited Abram.
It was just after I married him. King Nimrod,
inflamed by Abram's attitude, sent word.
So Abram came forward, to boast that *his* God could
quench even Nimrod's fires. Ox-headed Abram.

They threw Abram in the furnace. He walked on air.
Flames bloomed to a garden. Abram had the last word,
and I am glad I married Abram,
against all common sense. And even now,
when life in Ur has gotten so dangerous for us,
Abram's Holy One says, "Get thee *out!*"

And so we go.

Landed and Dispossessed: giving the bride away

Shechem, Moreh, Bethel, Ai, Hebron, Moriah, on and on. . . . Our routine: haShem's altar first, my tent, then his, then Lot's; local bargains, small cattle pastured; please haShem, let this stay be long. It never is. Welcome wears and I begin to learn arrival and possession are frames of mind; leave-taking is half of greeting.

For Abram there is nothing that is not a sign. At dawn, as we prepare to cross the Nile's seven arms into Egypt, I kneel by the stream to wash the night of weeping from my face. I hear a gasp behind me, turn to see Abram staring at the surface where my face floats shattered by splash. "You're beautiful!" he shrieks, as if it were my fault. "We must hide you or Pharaoh will kill me to have you." Never mind that travel is bad enough without traveling in the dark, I crouch down in our largest trunk, to cross into Egypt as simple cargo. I suppose I should be flattered, but I don't know. . . .

At last the bearers thud my casket down at the customs gate. "What's in here?" A rapping stills my breath. "Barley," says my husband's voice, far away. "We think it's more than that." Abram offers to pay the tax on wheat, if only they will not look. On silk. On pepper. What am I worth my weight in? Abram offers to pay the tax on rubies, if only. . . . That does it. They force the lock. I stand. I look at Abram. He does not look back. "She is my sister," he says, "and if your Pharaoh should want her. . . . "

Seeing Through: an exodus

> I tell Pharaoh to send my "brother" pearls and sheep,
> slaves, oxen, precious metals, all commodities
> that, unlike me, are not too good to keep.
>
> I am supposed to marry Pharaoh, but he gets sick.
> I humor him and pretend to read his fever-dreams:

A Hermit: "A fish is amiss in mummy land . . . "
A Princess: (*Trailed by a fat little cloud, draws her sword.*)
The Hermit: "Death's in my hand like a fishhook."
The Princess: "Judgment lies at the hairline."
(*She slits the cloud-belly over Pharaoh's head.*)

Pharaoh feels himself dissolve and wakes in a sweat.

I opine: These plagues of yours are more than bad luck.
You see, I am the princess and my brother the hermit;
The little cloud is Abram's god, and I am Abram's wife.

If you let me go back to him, I'll make him say a prayer
to cure and thank you. All your troubles will be over.
Pharaoh's last gift to me is his daughter, Hagar.

A Gift for War: the thrift of love

What kind of wife would be eager for her husband to go to war?
Who understands the politics? who Amraphel and Arriwuku,
Chadortaomer, Beara of Sodom, or Birsha of Gomorrah are?
Word from Sodom to the oaks of Mamre: Lot's in trouble there.
So Abram must go to the rescue — it's his only nephew.
To worry — it's only natural.
                              So you sit and you wait for news.
They say the planet Zedek made a fog of weird light
all around Abram as he fought. Can you believe what you hear?
And that Layla — some kind of angel — let him see right
through her, and the swords of his enemies dissolved in air
like salt in water. You could see even their arrows evaporate.
But when Abram throws just a handful of sand, every grain
turns into a javelin!
                       Ah, but half of the things I hear
I don't believe. So they make up stories to keep up their spirit.
This I understand. I wonder — where was this magic in Egypt? War!
Who needs it?

And then, a woman likes to see a memento, a souvenir.
But listen — after all those nice victories, what does Abram do?
Bring home an expensive knickknack, as much as a candlestick? No.
Yet the King of Sodom himself, they say, said, "Take everything."
Only Abram has with haShem some kind of promise, not to.

One thing
I've learned from experience: never to pass up or to throw away
so much as a sandal thong or piece of camel's hair, worn linen,
used nails, apple cores, ashes . . . so there must have been
something he could have picked up — half a cloak buckle maybe,
a silk tassel . . . Now the last thing Abram needs, I know,
is a complaining wife; yet how can he come home all holier-than-thou
empty-handed? and not even thinking how I must have suffered?
Men do not often appreciate . . .

Still, I am very glad
Abram did not fall into a slime pit.

Bits and Pieces: a covenant of One and one

Then one day I am looking up the hill from my tent door
and there is Abram cutting in half his best heifer,
a ram and a nice nanny goat, the way he sometimes does
when other rich men come to settle some business.
You'd think he would mention it to me. He is all alone.
Naturally vultures come. He jumps up and down like a crazy man.

I say (I am not hiding that I am upset), "This is going too far.
Study, study, study. Without enough exercise, without fresh air,
ruining your only pair of eyes. So is it a big surprise
you fall down in a fit? Look at this bloody mess.
Tell me something — are you proud of this?"

"Oh, yes,
he says, "yes, yes, yes, yes, yes. The Holy One
has come to seal this covenant with me — He came in person —

6

and He promised me, my children, and their children and . . .
They are to be as many as stars or grains of sand."
    Infinity! So many. Who needs this?

Gifts and Gratitude: second thoughts about generosity

I

Talk about sacrifices! I do my best to believe
and do everything according to what haShem says
to Abram that we must do in order to conceive.

All day I am running from here to there —
and I am not as young as I used to be —
to fetch for the altar, to prepare, to prepare.

And then — may my ears fall off if it is not
true — I overhear my darling at his prayers:
"It were better I be childless," he says. *Than what?*

II

HaShem knows how
        I have suffered to be a good wife to you, Abram,
        and with moving every other week.
Who knows why?

I'm not so dumb.
        Don't think I can't, can't see the sly looks you give
        my maid Hagar — and she's no lambkin either —
I'm able to bear

the truth at least.
        Her child could be mine to raise, born on my knees
        by law, where wives run dry and husbands yearn
for second best.

So this is it.
I hope I am not a selfish person. What do I ask
in return? Gratitude? Listen, gratitude — I have had —
and I can do without.

III

Abram, listen. I thought I was too old
to change. I was wrong. My heart's not gold.
As I said, I didn't expect gratitude.

But I didn't expect to lose my face
to this slave's. Let's just get something straight.
This woman used to wash my feet.

Has she worried herself sick about your eyes?
Has she had to tell fibs and make sacrifices
to protect Your Majesty? What kind of a god is this

who makes one woman to put another down?
I hate myself for this. I set her hair on fire.
Sometimes I hear her cry at night, and I don't care.

Send her away for the sake of my soul.
I'm past the age when it's fun to be a shrew.
I am begging you.

A Very Hard Thing to Understand: a bloody husband

So Hagar left and things calmed down. HaShem called her back. She
kept her place, she shared her son, and that was that. Could I find
energy to care anymore? I should live so long. So imagine my surprise.
This one afternoon I am going out to get some water, and there is
Abram standing at his tent door with some of his cronies, all of them
swaying back and forth, as if in wordless prayer or toothache, biting
coarse camel blankets or sandal leather, some cupping hands between

their thighs. Abram is spotted all over with blood, thinking maybe I don't see the knife he's hiding. "Sarai . . . " he begins, "Sarai, just a little bit of skin . . . " The rest is mumbled. "You have cut your what?" "Sarai . . . haShem said . . . " "HaShem couldn't be satisfied, you offer to go childless for his sake, counting stars like an idiot? May the Shekinah sharpen her wings on your back, and do like this to your neck!"
Let me just say that this is a very hard thing
for me to understand.

One Plus One: union and separation

Mornings when Abram sings to his Sefer Yetzirah,
    Evenings when my love is in his mind's patterns,
Am I supposed to enjoy talking to myself? I do.
    Hermit plus serpent are two.

This is the union:
One by myself I make up the feeling of plus.
Sarai is small cattle princess, tent peg, flax.
Iscah is the eye of Eve, a sweet tooth, nakedness.
Sarai and Iscah are one with stylus in hand.

In creation proper no one is alone:
Elohim, Adam, Adamah are one.
Adamah, Eve, and Sarai are one.
Sarai and Iscah and laughter are one.
Iscah's book is made of scatterings all over.
The stories Sarai tells are one-day wonders.

This is the separation:
Abram sways with concentration in his tent;
Sarai plays with murmurs and stirs them in the soup.
Abram invents what to make of the alphabet;
Sarai weeps it out of shouts and laughs it inside out.

Iscah polishes sight with tears and cheers like wind in laurel.
He learns by head what she knows by heart.
So much for him.

A Stranger Mystery: sustaining hospitality

And I have to laugh the next day too, as long as I see
Abraham humming to himself, content in the dog-day sun
at his tent door. But then he leaps up, as the strangers — three —
approach. Nothing goads Abraham out of self-pity like someone
to entertain. He gestures madly, scampers out to meet them,
leads them back and makes them comfy under one of the oaks.
I know what's coming: "Sarah — three good measures — for cakes —
and hurry — they can't, can't stay all night."

                              A stranger is a Mystery,
as Abraham likes to say, blah, blah. . . .

    I don't want to complain, but to be honest, I don't feel so well today.
    Far be it from me, however, to spoil a party.
    So here I am, mixing the batter, setting it aside, shaking
    sour whey in a skin. And there is ridiculous Abraham —
    scarcely healed — running, fetching, carrying, worrying —
    just like a woman.   I bleed for him. . . .
                      Oh.
                      It is more than a metaphor —
    I feel . . . between my legs.   But the ember cakes! I have tainted them!
    How strange. It's been decades since I've stained a thing. I
    cannot serve them now. Abraham will wonder — and if I tell,
    about such a matter. . . .   I hear the men laughing.

I do not usually eavesdrop, but in an emergency . . .
One of the strangers is predicting Abraham's son,
my son, and in a year from now. Sure thing. I am ninety.
Abraham . . . is ninety-nine.
                Ha!
                I laugh.

I laugh behind the tent-flap —
to myself, I hope —
could they hear it?
I rush then into the quiet-as-death quiet . . .

"We were about to ask after you, Sarah,"
I look at their plates. "But now, have a cup of wine with us,"
says the one called Michael — I think it is —
                                    They are eating like birds, all of them.

I suggest a smidgen of this or that — or are they full
already? Maybe just some dates . . . a sliver of melon?
Some honey? They are not eating enough even to make
decent scarecrows. Maybe they were too busy talking.
I am not asking if they want any cake.

                    "What I came for,"
I turn to Abraham, "is to say I'm sorry, but the cakes
are not right for you to eat. By that I mean,"
        I turn to the guests, "my husband is allergic, not quite, but . . . "
Abraham coughs. I blush. And one called Raphael says,
        "Sarah, why did you laugh just now?"
                                    "Laugh?" I say,
"who laughed? The wind in that tree . . . ? Maybe Lilith . . . "
"But you did laugh," says Gabriel, staring through me.

        "All right, I heard you joking about us.
We are ninety and ninety-nine years old . . . "
                    "You laughed."
"Is it a nice thing to do, to tease an old man,
        and when he is being so generous?"
        (To be the mother of a multitude — it breaks me up.)
"So? So I laughed."
                    I laughed because I already knew. . . .
I blush again. Abraham's guests get up to go.
                    I bleed for him.

Memo: another reason

And I laughed because there I was,
between my names, between my times,
between my ears, between my eyes,
feeling the hum of my first seclusion
as when my mother's words were glossed
by my body's aching signature.
                    A man,
she said, would come to my hearth;
a child, she said, would give me birth.
And she told me about a woman's bone.

It was all invisible, save for the blood.
It was all intangible, save for the pain.
It was all inaudible, save for the laughter
as she told me what she would tell my father:

When he asks for you I will say
I have no child by the name of Sarai,
but I have dressed a strange woman today.

And together we laughed between ourselves,
beside ourselves, inside ourselves.
There we were, ready to hold our own,
men coming to their conclusions alone.

"And Sarah said, 'God has made laughter for me.'" (Genesis 21:6)

Back under Mamre's homey oaks,
one month to go, and I'm just a barrel
of laughs. I tremble — the original joke's
still on us.
            By a labor of laughter I manage
to push Isaac's perfect head between my blue-veined thighs
that once all Egypt wanted to praise.

Screams of laughter from all sides save me from
screaming alone as the body slips out whole
as a perfect quip, with its long long story behind it,
like an afterbirth on everybody's lips.
The midwife snuggles a bundle into my arms;
 not a giggle; his eyes are shut in the subtle perfect
 mirth of Adam's sleep. Incomprehensibly
 begotten, the pale alphabet etched indelibly
 on the still stretched papyrus of my belly
 invents the birthcry.

Proof and Plenty: an ingenious entertainment

The cachinnation pales, paroxysm fades
to pang, the mountain of me subsides,
and Abraham, bored by confinement, decides
to throw a party. Every viceroy and king in all
Palestine is invited, with wives and infants, to a ritual
Abraham says will be the final seal
on his fatherhood — no one will call him a sterile mule
the way King Og once did. Already little Isaac's
a spitting image of Abraham, except for one artificial
detail — and this is what Abraham plans to fix.

Eight days old, Isaac's in the middle
of our circle of gifts and guests' wonder.
As Abraham approaches his child a shocked murmur
ruffles the crowd. In his hand is a knife.

I know he does not mean to kill, but still . . .
The huge blade flashes in the sun
as it comes down between Isaac's kicking feet.
I am almost blinded to the sight
of blood, a tiny spurt like wine jumping out
of a cup set too quickly down.
And that's it.

The Difference between Submission and Giving Up: dressing Isaac

So then — just the three — a very happy family —
Isaac growing up — Abraham getting on — haShem cut out
my tongue if I lie — but He makes a fool out
of anyone he chooses — all right — I accept — but suppose
for a laugh — haShem says to Abraham, "Go jump in
the Dead Sea" — I can see Abraham filling his pockets
with stones already . . .

That look on his face . . . So haShem is giving him
ideas again — this time a birthday surprise for Isaac:
he gets to go with his father to learn with Shem and Eber —
services, divine names, etcetera — all right I say
if it's not too far — after all, he's only thirty-seven,
a late bloomer maybe, but smart — so it's about time he finds
how to be on his own — how difficult — and maybe to appreciate
someone to cook, to mend. But be careful I tell him — especially
women — bring her home first — and don't talk to strangers.

The last night — my son comes in my tent —
we sob together like children — "Don't worry about me —
an old woman — I've had my life — you see here? —
my Sabbath lamp, my ornaments — you find a good wife,
it's all hers — my blessing." Isaac hugs me again,
but I'm not fooled. I drag out the battered trunk,
the same I bumped across into Egypt in, hiding my light —
get out the robe Abimelech gave me in Gerar —
the one I wore to hide my big belly that year —
and I dress Isaac in it.

Just like a king he looks — only a little uncomfortable,
as anybody would with such a long journey — and I get out the cloth
I laid the table with for the three strangers —
that time I laughed, and I laugh again
to think — and I wrap it around Isaac's perfect head
against the sun, fasten it with the precious stone

Melchizedek gave to me — from Noah's wife.
So then in the morning — a little picnic basket —
meat and mustard, dates and my special ember-cakes —
the basket I'd carried out of Ur, a little frayed — a bride I was. . . .
"Have a good time," I say — "I don't mind staying home
all alone" — and to Abraham, "Don't let him carry
so much — he is loaded down like a mule already
with the firewood, and be sure and stop to rest —
and in shade — and eat — I will not have any son of mine
come home like a ghost of a ghost or with eyes like holes
burned in a blanket." I wave and wave.
I see them out of sight. I see them up to no good.
A mother can only do so much.

Out of Sight in Mind: delivery at Mount Moriah

So I wave and watch 'til they are small as grains
of sand, and as infinite to my mind.
I have aged more in the last nine hours
than in my ninety barren years.
Meanwhile second sight has grown with this second life.
The price is no more than innocence. It is not right
or wrong I can see, but inevitability.
Abraham sees so far into the distance
all closer things are blurred. HaShem save his eyes.
                    HaShem help his eyes.

My own eyes seem caught in the magic web
of Isaac's robe. After all, I lived in it
in the largest months of my life, and through
the robe I feel his movements now as I did then.
He moves to be finally free of me, step by step
beside his father's self-absorbing prayers.
My husband is determined to deliver a child
to haShem the only way he can, by giving up
some life that belongs to him. He does not understand.
                    He will not understand.

A woman does not understand any better
what makes life come from her and why she must
let go of it. But by labor and sacrifice
of a perfectly natural sort, she gives her gift without
losing sight of it. "Are you sure you want to
let him go?" Abraham said, wanting me to scream "NO"
and so free him from whatever promise. But it's not for me
to hold back consequences. "As I live,"
I said, and I meant it, "try me." And so he does.
                              And then he does.

As if my third eye were the jewel I fastened
so carefully on Isaac's turban, I see Moriah's peak.
The altar stacked where Cain and Abel tried
to nail down haShem's preference, where Adam
and Noah bound their dreams and bargains . . .
All altars are the same: highest follies charged
with hopes: over and over and over, the same ground . . .
Sacrifice happens naturally as the leaves fall
from trees, and if not, not. There is no general point.
                              There is no special point.

Shudders go through my body as if I wore
the flowing robe once more. The labor has begun.
How do I know? Some may say disguised Satan came
to tattle, as if he were a friend of mine!
Some may imagine an angel midwife-detective told.
But a woman knows: she knows. Her body is on the line.
The thought of Abraham binding me down to his promise
still strikes strange fire in my head and lets me see
over his busy shoulder. There must be another way.
                              There must be some other way.

It's something Abraham taught me long ago,
whether he knew it or not: that haShem believes
in metaphor. Behind the father and son, I see the dumb
ram struggling to speak. His trembling
I understand. In some way all things being
equal at the moment of death, the father turns
as if to an annunciation, able to hear the hum
of thoughts arising where his son begins to breathe
in relief, once more. The cord is cut. His eyes have cleared.

My eyes can shut.

I HEARED
DE ANGELS SINGIN':
HARRIET TUBMAN

Yes ma'am, de Almighty He make me
    dat kind of woman jump right up an' stand
        herself 'twixt some white devil man
an' dis poor bondman she know dat very day be set
    on his long run for it an' dat for to be
        free
an' I had a mind to join up wid him
    but den de Lord He see fit
        for to fix my head plumb where
de weight de white man hurl in wrath
    done hit an' it like to bust
        my skull an de soul fly out.

Dey might to left me lay
    but I be worth cash money —
        strong critter like me — an' a load o' sweat.
Master he let my mama nurse me gentle
    back from dat throb of dark
        an' ever since dat time
from out of dis hurted head de fits an' de visions
    come on me an' sure I be blessed
        to hear de angels sing, see 'cross dat line
to where my freedom life stretch out its hand.
    An' I be mighty blessed
        by anger too: when I thinks how *she* whip me
            for a mite of dust
        right out of de big house, how *he* loan me out
            to plow . . .

Times come dis heavenly power
    jus' come clean through me an' I knows for sure
        de Lord is in me to take my peoples through
            de tribulations of de railroad North
jus' like I do.
    I got me eyes
        for de dead of night an' ears
            for de leastest whispers.
        I got me nerves
an' dey flitters like a snake's tongue,
    tick for to tell me
        where de death-dangers be hidin' out.
            It be like to de ways my papa knowed
                to prophesy on weather.
            I got me secret ways.

Den de times do come I jus' gets emptied out
    like to a rain barrel sprung a leak.
        De air it go spirit-pale an' chill
            as a whipp'd child's heart
                an' I seems to fall
down through some vast an' be landed in a sleep
    nobody can't wake me from but de Lord Hisself
        when he goes to set dem angels singin'
            in dis hurted head of mine.

                    • • •

First time I runs off
myself all by my lonesome
I done heared about de so-called railroad
     to freedom
               but I didn't have no notions of whereabouts
               dem railroad tracks nor stations be.
So I jus' clinches my eyes. . . .
I done pray
     an' limps my way along to liberty
     an' when I comes to cross
dat magic line at last, I feels dis fear,
     I looks hard at my poor hands
     to see if I be de same person,
a person on de far side, free.
A stranger in a strange land
     sure enough an' real soon I got me friends
          who knowed de railroad up an' down.
I got me work an' some cash money. . . .
                              So I saves
an' I asks an' I ponders de ways to go.
     an' I sneaks back over
          dat magic line.

Nineteen times I makes dis journey down
     an' somewheres along de way
          I get me de name Moses. . . .
               dey says how I might could part de waters
               an' dry up swamps for my peoples to march on through,
               how I might could lick a white slavecatcher
               barehanded, smell dem devils out
               two counties away, how I falls into my trance
               for to speak wid de very angels
               in de Celestial City
               how I feeds my passengers
               manna when de pickins is low
               how when I'm 'bout to commence a raid
               I'm like to turn plumb invisible!

. . .

Truth be, I gets my orders from de Lord.
    Then sly as a cat in long grass I snugs me close
        by de Quarter an' commence my song:
           Who dat yonder all dressed in red?
                I heared de angels singin'.
           It look like de childrens Moses led,
                I heared de angels singin'.
    An' I knows dey knows an' dere hearts be turnin'
        yonder towards de praise-grove
           where each alone come sneakin'
                an' each come alone all roundabout
to hark for de whippoorwill in de dark
    dark as blackstrap; an' dark dere lonesome shadows
        kneelin' down 'twixt dem stones
           tiltin' all whichways over de restin' souls
           we be leavin' behind.
I whistles out the whippoorwill again
    an' dey be all gatherin' round an' shiverin'
        an' Canada seem 'bout as far as Heaven.

. . .

Bad off by dawn we be hunkered down
    in some wet ditch done prickled by de rough
        pine boughs we lays like a blessin' over us.
Come nigh dusk, an' if my heart beat safe
    I creeps out as I knows traps and scavengin'.
        I finds us maybe a windfall
        old walnuts, some moldy cobs
        lyin' round in de tumbled stalks
        or it comes to pass de Lord give me
        to catch us a woodchuck or squirrel.

. . .

"Where we be, Moses?"
　　　　(An' dey be like to cuss me.)
"Somewheres in Creation, on our way,"
　　　　I says an' I knows
　　　　　　　　in my bones dey be like to commence a ruction
　　　　　　　　　　be like to call down de horsemens
　　　　　　　　　　　　'pon us wheres we be hid.
I takes my stand den, I stands up
　　　　to dem doubters.
　　　　　　　　　　　　"You been worse off," I says,
　　　　　　　　　　　　"You been bondfolk."

· · ·

And blessed be Levi Coffin an' Gerrit Smith
an' Thomas Garrett — two thousand souls passed through
　　　　his hands on de way to freedom — God bless dem all.
An' blessed be Frederick Douglass an' good John Brown.
　　　　('Fore I ever meets dat man de Lord show me a vision
　　　　where de serpent eats him up.)
　　　　　　　　I done my best.
An' I nurses dem wounded Union mens
　　　　wid potions my mama's mama teached her to fix
　　　　　　　　from roots an' leaves.
I washes so many wounds one day
　　　　I be washin' blood wid thinner blood
　　　　　　　　'til I thinks I be washin' all dem in de blood
　　　　　　　　of de Lamb where de bloods all do mix.
　　　　　　　　Praise Him.

· · ·

An' now what be happenin'
　　　　is my friends is gettin' after dem high hats
　　　　　　　　down at Washington, askin' what dey gonna do
　　　　　　　　　　for dis old woman done so much.
I don't say nothin'.

Dey comes to me for to hear de mysterious ways,
for to hear my storytellin', for to be a-singin':
Who dat yonder all dressed in blue?
I heared de angels singing.
It look like de childrens jus' come through,
I heared de angels singin'.

"Where we be now, Moses?"
An' I answers slow,
"Don't you worry you none.
It be a long ways to go yet,
here ain't no Heaven
but we be somewheres in Creation
on our way."

LESSON FROM
THE COTTON MILLS OF LOWELL

If it is said that many a one has here found a grave,
shall it not also be said that many a one has here found
the path to heaven?

— *The Lowell Offering*, October 1845

I.

Don't cry, Florilla, you know you aren't the first
to come homespun to Spindle City, find
yourself quite lost. The first day is the worst,
what with its solitude of ceaseless sound,
the overseer with his eye on you,
the trembling floor that hoggles all your bones;
you think that you will never learn to do
so much as doff a bobbin where time spins
round and round, unending snarl. I know
you miss Vermont, the quiet hills at dawn,
the farm, the family . . . Just think of how
your sacrifice will make it so your brother can
go to college. Meanwhile the mill will be
your school. You'll find yourself. You'll see.

II.

The thunder, buzz and hiss and whiz, the whirr
of pulleys, rollers, spindles, flyers, wheels . . .
it's crickets, frogs, and Jew's harps all together.
They are inside of me. I'm dragged by bells
from dawn 'til dusk. I am a single part
in one living machine, this work of threads
and circles, harness, hammer, springs. The heart

beats to the river ripping past and needs
nothing now but livelong friction. Still,
there's darkness in the loom. There is the lure
of madness, too, Tamar, a heaven-hell,
as voices weave themselves within the roar . . .
The mill rears high to the belfry; the sky is blood;
innumerable windows glitter, but the grounds . . . are mud.

III.

Forget those darknesses, Florilla, think
how bees gather honey from a poison flower,
and of our Sundays rambling, the mill-race bank,
wild roses tumbling, columbine clinging, where
we hear the bluebells ring . . . Those hours contain
our "alphabet of angels," meaningful
as our Improvement Circle, where we learn
to speak as the city speaks and see the mill
as a moral lesson: how the whole world works
by singing clatter, where bells and threads converse
in a finished fabric, love. The mill wheel's spokes
ceaselessly turn and drip, the hidden source
of everything. "The worm on the earth may look
up to the star." The circle, God's gravity, our work. . . .

IV.

A sin, Tamar? Where the spindles sing long yarns,
air steamed and windows shut, to think of Joan
whose work was menial, how while her arms
embraced a mindless service, she was alone
with unearthly messengers, her bonds undone
by hovering wings . . . They tell me that I am
the Gospel's handmaid as I weave . . . Eve span,
like me, from Genesis to Bethlehem . . .
Meanwhile, the lords of spade and shovel squat
in shanties and Hog Latin mucks the pure
syllables in my brain. On Merrimack Street
the devil's in needle books and ginger beer
and pavement Romeos. Joan burned for Charles
crowned. I hear you, angels, as my poor thread snarls

and I shall take my life and lay it down
in Pawtucket Falls, at the foot of the mill rearing high
to the belfry full of bats and the setting sun,
where the million windows glitter and speak to me.

POCAHONTAS:
FROM HER NEW WORLD

I. *To Powhatan*

Dear, great Powhatan, father, I would write
news to you of this new world, and yet,
the deepest syllables that I might use
are nowhere written. There's no alphabet
between us, only the sound low as the tide
in a shell's throat —
(My husband John surprises me. "What's this?"
he asks me. "Is the Princess Pocahontas
not satisfied, the royal belle of London,
but she must scribble, too, and prove the savage
can compete with Shakespeare?" I insist
I am but writing for my father. "Ha!"
quoth my husband. "Do you think Powhatan
is learning so much English in your absence?"
"His tongue has not the script nor words I need,"
say I. "It is a letter for myself.
I feign it is for him so I may say
what else I might not say of what I see."
"You've learned to talk in riddles," says John then. "I fear
you may have learned the use of words too well.
Yet go on." He chucks my chin. "But for you
King James would not approve our sweet tobacco.")

>   (I carry a small light globe inside of me
>   at the center of my body and as I move
>   it steadies my senses, still, among snail shells
>   and silk grass, back straight and belly flat,
>   stringing cranberries on nettle fiber,
>   scooping light into dolls of clay or wood . . .)

The Earl of Buckingham is next to me
in the royal box. The Globe is full.
There's Jessica and Juliet together,
somehow sharing the center of my dream
of infinite translations . . . Do I love
a loathed enemy? . . .
I must work to understand some jokes.
Prince Charles explains: the maidens, fish and weapons,
bitten thumbs, the have-at-thee's and down-
with-those, the flourishes and purple fountains . . .
In sooth, I know not why I am so sad . . .
Did I deny my father and refuse my name?

       (I see Powhatan standing on the shore
       as, flag-strung and square-rigged, we float away
       from the spume-flecked dunes. We each grow small in each
       other's eyes. His sadness is moon-faced . . .)

The Earl of Pembroke quaffs the fume and chats
throughout the play — he's all embroidery,
pompons and glitter, gold-clocked hose . . . I see
Tomocomo in his beads and feathers
play his part, clay-daubed, proud of his crown
of snake and weasel skins . . . while I dress up
in shoes that pinch and petticoats and velvet
crushed. Who's best on stage? These daughters leave
their fathers, all for love . . .

       (I have not forgotten how to stitch with bone,
       make porcupine and oyster stew. I long
       for my bed of pine boughs in Virginia, long
       for the clean river at dawn, my skin
       open to Ahone: I long for my clearing,
       the trees mothering at the edge, the moon washing down,
       my father's voice . . .)

I cannot hear you say my baptized name:
Rebecca, Lady Rebecca Rolfe . . . I ask
one of King James' translators what it means,
Rebecca: it means *to bind,* means *beautiful*
as animals noosed for sacrifice: that is,
binding as a promise . . . binding as blood, my own
mixed with my husband's in Thomas' veins.
You see, I do not like a strict translation.
"Pocahontas" means more than your playful wanton.
It means to risk, means to explore the world,
to dress as for a play and play it out
so far as beasts bound in crinolines and lace
can play, and this brings peace, as my baptism
did, to Jamestown and your warriors,
if not to me. I dream of no return.

I rave, the London air has poisoned me.
The sea between us is the vast between
myself and myself. . . .
You let me go . . . You stood there on the shore . . .
How does one piece the old and new together
but by separations, explorations
in the crossing of two strains, the grief and joy
that makes one wild to see the ends of things
and the beginnings that are the ends of words
between us, father, where
I am Pocahontas, wanton; Rebecca, bound;
and something else, not old or new, but found.

II. *To Captain John Smith*

Dear Captain Smith, they told me you were dead,
and I believed, despite my deeper sense
that we would meet again, and here you are

in London. Badly dressed and bungling
your apologies for leaving me
with no farewell . . .

(John Rolfe is looking over my shoulder again.
"Another letter? When you should rest yourself!
Aren't the deaths of half your retinue
of 'Naturals' enough to frighten you?"
He puts his careful hand against my cheek.
"You're burning up! Or is this blush because
your letter, as I note, is for John Smith,
that antagonistic foolish man.
His creditors will get him yet, you know."
"It is a letter for myself," quoth I,
"it's not for him or you or anyone . . . "
"Go on, but if I hear you cough once more,
I'll take your quill and ink away for good.")

Some called you hero, some impostor, I —
I still recall the horror on your face,
you who brag of being a soldier to the Prince
of Transylvania, so worldly-wise,
when you came upon our harvest dance,
the maidens naked but for bells and paint
dancing the ring of fire, and led by me.
Oh, yes, I had my eye on you that night.
We sit and suck sweet cobs together, you
teach me new words: for *food,* for *dance,* for *moon.*
We do not touch. Your eyes are shifty, bright.
I smell your skin, your fear. I want to tease
you as I tease my brothers. Some called you hero.
That was my innocence. Not long before
I had been waiting for my womanhood
away from men, in the long house of the maidens.
Free, I find my way to Wingandacoa
through moonflowers, flaming foxglove, whortleberries.
I am the eyes between the leaves. I listen
for more than rabbit, porcupine, and fox.

I listen for strange words: *to starve, to die.*
I see your secret burials. I pity you,
God's handful, eating your bitter bread, but most
I want my wizard Smith to hold his own,
the man of mirrors, thunders, man of words.
So I bring food and I bring warnings, too,
through snow and bramble, against Powhatan's will.
And then you're gone, wounded, so they say,
and in disgrace. They tell me you are dead.
It was not for that, my grief; my grief
was that you were no more than other men.
But it is foolish to discuss such lies,
now I am John Rolfe's wife and Thomas' mother.

And still, and still, I have to know one thing.
It's whispered here in London, you have told
how Powhatan meant to sacrifice
your life, and when your head was on the stone,
Pocahontas flung herself upon you,
took your head in her arms and saved your life.
Did you dream it?

> (I recall the dream. It made me blush,
> forbidden as I was to touch a man,
> much less a *tassentasse.* And yet your hair,
> so coarse and wild with firelight, face
> so hot, the sense of your whole trembling form
> stretched out — the power, vulnerability
> stayed with me many days. I told no one.
> I was ashamed, and rapt.)

                                    You are so changed.
And I am changed. I am a Lady now.
I've been to Whitehall, Hampton Court, masked balls.
And you are something faded, out of touch.
I don't want our dream, and yet I do.
And even now, I want to hide. I want
to hate what pulls me out of myself, away

from the wildwood's quiet, beginning with that dream
that is not mine alone, that makes me seem
sometimes hero, sometimes impostor, just like you.
You funny man, you fallen thing, what a tangle
of worlds you have brought me to, and what an end . . .
of masquerade, toys, powers, enmities
and surprising peace, dear impostor, dear friend.

III. *To John Rolfe*

Dear Husband, when you thought to marry me
despite your aweful trembling at the thought
of God's displeasure with the sons of Levi
for marrying strange wives —

> (Can I not sit down with quill and ink
> but John must come and read my stiff beginning?
> "What have you got to say to me that you
> must write it out, ill as you are?"
> "I must write because I'm going to die.
> I must fashion coherent memory,
> these years have gone so fast." I bite
> my tongue to keep from crying out to him
> to save me, but there's nothing he can do.
> "I've had a dream," I say, "my father was
> on the Pamunkey shore scattering beads
> among my people. I lay wrapped in doeskin
> with food and water for the journey, pearls,
> and my little mirror. I saw my brothers blacken
> their faces and howl . . . " "Tell me no dreams," says John,
> "of savage things. You are in London now,
> a Lady, blessed, beloved of God and me.
> Remember this, if you must write." He turns
> and goes. I hear the sob caught in his throat.)

What a lot we had to teach each other.
Remember how I came to Henrico, bound
as hostage, dressed in unfamiliar clothes,
preached to in a language I not yet
fully understood. I asked myself,
was I stolen or did I give myself?
And then I met you at the Jamestown Church.
I carried my hornbook with its alphabet
and Lord's Prayer. You asked the Reverend
if you might help me with the catechism.
Why was I created? You had to ask yourself
as much as I. Had Satan struck your heart
with his hot hoof? I knew I lay between
your God and your secret heart; your dusky love,
your persimmon, your godly tax, your dream
that wakes you to astonishment, still,
as God takes you by the hand and you take mine.

> (I stand before the altar in my Dacca muslin,
> the same I wore to be baptized Rebecca,
> Powhatan's absence as a wound in me,
> Powhatan's gift of freshwater pearls around
> my neck, a white ivory comb in my hair,
> and with my body I thee worship, said
> and done, the "Peace of Pocahontas," done.)

I told you when to tap the maple tree.
You showed me the tiny Trinidado seed.
I told you in which thickets the turkeys hid.
You taught me how to spin, make cheese and candles.
I showed you roots and leaves and barks that heal.
I knew migrations, spawnings; you knew books
and theater. We planted corn and beans
in the same plot, together, crossed our strains . . .

You see how Thomas likes his wooden hoop
and hobbyhorse. He is as English as
he is Powhatan. Do you recall the verse
in Genesis: "And the Lord said unto her,
Two nations are in thy womb." The name
Rebecca is truly mine . . . It is enough the child
lives, to return my blood to Virginia's shore.
All my dreams are departures now, just as
my life . . . I feel as swift and deep and wide
as the Thames, I loop past Greenwich, Halfway Reach,
past the chalky cliffs of Gravesend where . . .

> (. . . hedgerows blossom, and lilacs. Prince Charles calls
> me sister, I understand his burdens well . . .
> I am a work of grief and cambric . . . hold me.)

You say this is a julep of unicorn's horn,
powdered with pearl and a stag's heart bone?
It's useless, my love, it is a fairy tale.
I am beyond and beyond myself, sweet John,
I hear the bells of St. George toll . . . Is this
once more the Twelfth Night Masque where dreams have wings
and dreams have honey and dreams have stings all come
from a moving cloud and bower of flowers
breaking open inside of me . . . I go . . .
go out upon the sea where nothing is
written, but the thought becomes a wave
in a lack-brain turbulence . . . where nothing is
spoken above the wind that blows beyond
myself and beyond myself I balance, ride
a sleep of sad motions and an edge
of piercing beauty, of kneeling in moonlight
where I am yet to be stolen, given away,
where my father and my husband and my son
kneel beside *the mother I must have had,*
her arms around and around and around me now. . . .

CONCORD'S CHILD:
LOUISA MAY ALCOTT

for Elizabeth Hadas

Do you want to know the real Louisa May?
Does one exist? Right now she's folding pink
flannel penwipes in the hospital
where Dr. Rhoda Lawrence oversees
her naps and drops, massage and baths.
                                        My bones
throb, my right thumb's paralyzed for good
from pressing down on moral pap, my voice
is froggy, all the hurts I've ever had,
the vertigo, dyspepsia, rheumatic pains,
come back in force. I shiver in my furs.

Everything must have its meaning in the end,
if only I can rearrange. I need to search
my diaries, my letters. I destroy
and add, but what's the use — the truth is still
unsayable. One story of my life
was started as "Success"; it ends as "Work,"
and as in *Little Women*, something's lost.
Is it the mysterious key, the one that springs
the vortex in my brain where duchesses,
evil-hearted actresses, grandees,
banditti, nuns, sylphs, orphans, suicides,
opium eaters, artists, wretches, all
the elements of temperament, release
the plots and counterplots behind a mask
worn to please?

Oh, Papa, let me please
you; Marmee, let me follow all the steps
to Concord's transcendental home, if not
to your Celestial City. I admit
impatience, selfishness and willfulness,
independence, vanity and pride,
not to mention love of cats — it's here
in this old diary from Fruitlands days.

Dressed in linen, scrubbing, grubbing, crowded
by visiting idealists, dubious,
we eat our pure and bloodless solar meals
of water, graham bread, apples, wholesome nuts,
gossiping of gross Brook Farm. It's hard
to be the daughter of experiments,
take cold baths and keep a diary
for inspection, nod through clouds of talk
of moral kingdoms, Edens, Genius . . .
Dark, demonic, no child of my father's light,
somehow a freak, a girl-boy, wild and queer,
born carnivore with lurid tendencies,
I dreamed gigantic loves . . . How could I translate
misery to goodness, then?
                                  There was that dream —
that I returned alone to Concord, searched
for Orchard House, dear Apple Slump, but found
a great gray castle there instead, of stone,
with towers and arches, antique bridges. . . . No one
knows me. Someone says he sold the place
to Mr. Alcott. Where did he get the means?
"From his daughter, it seems, the one who died
ten years ago." A ghost, then. I watch small boys
run through the grounds with Father, young and plump.
I nod to him, but he can't recognize. . . .
I catch myself in a mirror, all fat and gray;
I slip away.

I never dreamed I'd play
so many parts, betray so many lives:
"Tribulation Periwinkle" in
a ballroom full of deathbeds, tending wounds;
"Flora Fairfield" writing moral scraps
and "A. M. Barnard" bringing in the cash
with tales Louisa Alcott could not sign.
And one of me is rich, one destitute,
one staid, one reckless, one anonymous
in passion's vortex; one is named "Aunt Jo,"
grown-up tomboy, topsy-turvy; plus,
the made-up boys I might have been or loved.

Mostly the dead preside in Concord now:
Mr. Hawthorne, mysterious and shy,
and Mr. Emerson, to whom I wrote
all those unsent letters, to whose Goethe
I played Bettina, leaving sheafs of flowers
on his next-door stoop; and Margaret Fuller, draped
in Grecian folds for conversation's sake;
and most of all . . . but how can I speak of him?
I must: my homely, manly Henry, gruff
and shaggy, tender to the child I was. With him,
I saw the tanager set the woods on fire,
heard woodthrush philosophies of goldenrod.
We spotted Indian arrowheads, otters' tracks,
found high bush blueberries, prunella flowers,
tickled the lizard, rowed on Walden Pond.
Some called his silence rude, some said he ate
asparagus from the "wrong" end. To me, his bluntness
seemed honesty. Even his coldness excited me.
Gloomed eyes under the old straw hat, broad shoulders tense
inside his checkered shirt. He let me touch
his flute and raise his spyglass to my eye.
I lost him when I ceased to be a child.
(It was no secret women tired him out.)

Before I took myself to Washington
to nurse our Union boys and learn firsthand
the male anatomy, Thoreau was dead.

Papa, my life has paid your debts, my hand
now smooths the white hairs on your head, my pen,
that once refused to write your life (of the cost
of living for Idea's sake), moves now
according to your will, your dream, your faith
in "American Genius" . . . If you'd had a son . . .
I did my best, no genius, it's true.

When I came home from Washington
to a house that seemed to have no roof, a house
where no one knew me in my delirium,
you let my fury be. My room was full
of men, and one, a wicked Spanish duke
in velvet, black, my spouse, stood over me,
leapt from closets, in at windows . . . I
appealed to the Pope in imaginary Latin,
was burnt as a witch and went to a boring Heaven,
but you brought me back as you've always brought me back
to myself — ungothic Louy, daughter, loved.

But somehow that's outside, outside of me.
And blood and thunder — that's outside me too.
Clocks and smiles and smiles and clocks — now why
do those words come to me as summary?
I have found time for everything and smiled
my way through poverty and gala teas,
Oversoul and oysters, John Brown hanged,
Van Ambergh's New Great Golden Menagerie,
the telltale mist that rose from Lizzie's corpse,
playing Mrs. Jarley on the stage,
the little women at Vassar tearing lace
from my gown for keepsakes, Mrs. Bliss
and her magnetic trances, Boston burned,

Flower Fables, women's causes, May's
death, Marmee's, May's child in my arms,
Mr. Emerson's barn and the summerhouse
of willow wands, picnics at "Spiderland,"
that bridesmaid's dress that seemed sackcloth and ashes,
the Polish boy who hated the Russian baron
while I hated the Virginia colonel at Vevey,
being revolutionary and . . .
                              American, certainly.
At any moment I expect to hear
of Papa's passing. Once he told me: act
just as if each day were someone else's
birthday. We've shared our birthday ever since
the day I was born. It's hard to realize
that I am I, and my parents coincidence . . .
Papa said, and I never understood,
"Life is the dispersion of the identities
and the concentration of the diversities."
Platonic balloon?
                          A child comes to the door
of Orchard House. She mourns: "I thought you would
be beautiful." I can't be everything.
I live on gluten gruel now, gems and cream.
Father wears my glasses instead of his.
Sometimes knows me, sometimes not, like me.
I smile. My sister's daughter comes to me
for a story and I spin something out
of Concord's childhood, thinking of the bird
that set the woods on fire, the flowers that spoke,
and while my lips are moving, I
watch the shadow lengthen by my chair.

EURYDICE

Born — Bridalled — Shrouded
In a Day
Tri Victory

"My husband" — women say —
Stroking the Melody —
Is this — the way.

— Emily Dickinson

I walk out —
walk out on my wedding day,
         on my wedding day to be
accosted by a serpent
                    in long grass —
He strikes — my body
         my body throbs — death's negligee,
seamless, slack replaces —
              replaced — my wedding dress.

I drift open — unbound until my nerves
resplice with old aches answering his song . . .

"Oh, Orpheus, let me be . . . "
                    He must observe
the rule he cannot see:
                    Me, as I tag along
behind — dumb dimwit ghost —
                    I have no choice
between self-serving light and self-same dark — the snake
was kindly quick, but here, this. . . .
              Hear this — a deathless voice
rend peace — "I'm ravished"
              "I'm ravished" — I hiss. "Just look —
I'm done for." He turns.
         He turns — away. This is the way.   *Damn hymn.*
Mad hags will someday tear him limb from limb

                              from limb

                                   from limb.

*P*LAIN LISA

for Alice Quinn

> *See that when you are drawing and make a beginning of a line*
> *that you look over all the objects that you are drawing for any*
> *detail whatever which lies in the direction of the line that you*
> *have begun.*
> — Leonardo da Vinci, *Notebooks*

I.

Leonardo's studio! Each time it takes my eyes
a while to settle down — one jot in all that
litter, too much to see — his planned obscurity
pulling up a lid, widening an iris'
black port to take in the giant wing-frames
hung from rafters, tubulous probes and calipers
set to track the sky or bedog the joints of flies,
his prize split human head for the moment
shelved, its tongue aloll; then, all
the live models — pretty boys, lutanists, jesters;
his caged doves, tame doe, fountain-fall.

By now I expect the mid-sitting breaks,
his sudden whim to drop the brush, take up
the knife for a quick dissection, peeling
an ear or elbow, careful cleaving to bare
bone from mauve muscle; I follow along
as he fingers a taut white tendon,
another exposed connection.
Luckily these sessions were all Francesco's
idea, so he can hardly object to the odd
evenings or rainy afternoons
Leonardo chooses to have me pose.

I don't mind a chance to get out of the house.
All in all, of what my master separates,
the eyes seem most incessantly perplexing.
Sometimes, as he paints, I find my own eyes
fixed on an apprentice behind him, propping
a fresh cadaver's face in view. The boy's
thumb and finger spread the bloodless eyelids
apart, tenderly insert themselves, as if
to pinch a plum from a tart, gently
to pull the soft sphere loose. He spits
to glisten it, and slowly, then, invites
his master to turn from me, see his prize rolled
in candlelight. As Leonardo stares
and stares to get his reflections right,
I dare to close my eyes. What with the focus
so everywhere at once . . . he may be a little
crazy as some say he is. I don't know . . .
I have to smile, though . . .

II.

When I agreed to this I didn't know how
long he'd keep me sitting on the edge of my chair.
And now it's been four years. The odd thing is
the longer he goes on the more there's left to do.

More angles keep coming into it, you see.

Not just a portrait for a blank space Francesco
wanted once to fill on our dining-room wall, it's also
what we talk about now, and the background music
as well as the trash and relics, jokes and tea.

And what is the use of hurry in eternity?

He has taught me how perfection is made
of perfect puttings off, conclusive inconclusions,
as when the viol and voice might stop but trade
and vary the phrase, instead, go on.

It's good to have our whole reserve, he tells me.

I like the riddles, puns, philosophy, fables;
to hear how I am only one of a number
of other experiments, my scatterbrain chatter
just one more raw material. His prime dream-question:

What does a person need, beyond curiosity,
to light the natural caverns of the brain?

III.

Leonardo smiles at my knack for silly notions.
I can't help smiling, too. But then,
"Stop it, Lisa, I can't see
past the stupid light edged on your teeth —
it glitters, something animal . . ."

He means we should avoid what may seem to be
the sin of explicit pleasure.
Ours is a serious business, after all . . .

> *where twilight is our perfect light*
> *and shadows a kind of wine,*
> *pale iris my flower, most Florentine,*
> *my white hands feeding the white*
> *tame doe white bread between the hours*
> *of sitting still still still and still*
> *with Sister Camilla my saintly friend*
> *in the corner mumbling her prayers*
> *who may well think we are unholy*
> *for all I know in this twilight where*

I grow more twin to my portrait each dim day,
and feel him looking out of my eyes as well
as into his dreams of shipwrecks and Cyprian hollows,
mechanics, poisons, planets, monsters, prophecy . . .

I may not be following exactly, but plainly
I am much more curious, as he treats me
like one of the boys, and tells me . . . but
about some things, I keep my mouth shut.

IV.

One night, not long ago, outside a storm
and all the candles lit in here — his favorite
shapes of light, a sudden bolt of pain
shot straight across the roof of my mouth,
up through my ear. I felt ready to join
the buzzing corpses piled in the other room.
So that was it.
My teeth came out.

And after that, when I came to sit,
"Damn it! the lines are gone, your jaw's a flop."

I freeze and watch as one by one he pries
uncoffined beggars' mouth-holes open, looks
for the odd whole tooth to match my bite, my lip;
and fastens the borrowed filed-down bits
with copper bands and wires them down my throat
to the ears of my heart.
My mouth was filled.
And that was it.

I thought he wouldn't give up.
Except for the pain, I would have smiled.

Francesco of course refuses to pay for this pale
and frankly unamusing reflection
of spousal glamour. He has filled the empty wall
with Piero's cartoon of a martyred donkey-angel.
Its placement, I think, is perfection.
When Leonardo had to leave all of a sudden
for France, he took me with him —
and that does make me, more and more . . . have to smile.

BOX-CAR BERTHA

I like the sneaky sound of it: transient, transient,
born transient, transient born: transient:
What does *transient* say but how it sees
more all of the bughouse, rat joints, shimmy-de-fer
the planet's alive with, your scrambles, headenders,
boneyard hassles, hustle or go nuts, 'cause you're on
the lam and foxing it like always, always hungry . . .

Surely God spoke too soon when he called this
baby, this seven-day wonder of his, and all that,
"good"? Eye-catching, though, it surely is:
with dogs and their angels hitting cinder together,
with plush-runs and wild-cats rattle-bashing through
the gandy-dancer's wake or greaseball's crapshoot.
Everything is there to see and moving too.
Sit still and the seasons just don't change as fast.
You've got the twitches so you travel.

Luck like mine is born by the steel and bo park,
grows up in wild hiding and seeking all life long
between the freights and the jerkwaters —
candy trains, hot shots, night owls and danglers,
worm drags, black snakes, the odd caboose-bounce . . .
and, for a shout, the glories among them.
Glories, the empty ones, crates big as churches.

One of my men thinks — can't pin me down — that I think
God's hiding in some boxcar. Like Hell.
But once I met this saint — trilby, top half of a tux
plus pajama bottoms, that God could do worse than
ape for the sake of fellow-feeling.
This whanger was thumping out bless-yous and curling
amens with a vengeance, supposedly,

at a gaggle of bundle stiffs gabbing by the switch.
I knew he was doing it double-barreled for me.
For me to witness and get cheered up by —
it's a funny thing, how easy it is to tell
redemptioneering from hell-bent kinkiness.
I was all for a gedunking in the river.
And after that, we got along quite swell.

My song: "Hobo Hobo where did you come from?"
The Wabash Cannonball, your dromomaniac's dream —
As a kid I was missing and every time they found me
(so they say) in some sidetracked X — i.e. crate,
brownie, house car, box — all the glorious same,
and hence the name, from Box-Car to Hotbox
Bertha — ha ha — All the same . . .
And meanwhile, Yours Truly has had the careers
like crazy: hobo, moll-buzzer, "they" of sorts,
typist for the occasional
lettuce, prossy, revolutionist (of sorts),
and have I ever (you bet!) seen all
the moving misfits anyone could want to spill
the short line griefs to, and now
I'm spilling the beans to you Professor
Doctor Dear — please, be my ghost.
I'll turn myself inside out while you sling some ink
on the depictures and explaterations,
brass tacks, breakdowns, chuckles,
turnips and such.
            Say, here's a story —
an arresting tale, so to speak —
there was this guy Big Otto, and we were in this
more or less confidence game — what mob monotony! —

and they wouldn't go soft so my sweet
conjuneero grifter cat bandit
and accidentally killer got nabbed and then
there's me knocked up with his baby
(accidentally).
                    So I could tell about how,
when I go to Otto's hanging to say good-bye and I'm not
as big as the Roseland Ballroom yet,
and just at the awful moment Otto drops
some little kicks are saying hello in my belly.
Wow.
                    How's that for an ending?
I couldn't think of a name,
so I always called her just plain Baby Dear.
And then I gave her away to some people who
could think of a name for her.

Another time, I worked for a "coffee and" pimp —
you don't know the type I'm sure —
and I learned the code of this place, the Globe Hotel:
the "good man" was a Friday, the $5 and $10 ones
were Holiday and Double Holiday respectively.
Yeah, holidays. Glories, in their way.
But hardly a one of them took off his shoes.
And for fun, there were plenty of narrow escapes,
mad dashes to the roof, so naturally,
sooner or later they get you, stick you in the kitty
to diddle and fiddle, maybe knit a sweater.
But what's all bad about a hit in the birdcage?
You make friends — cold hands, hoisters, door-matters,
skin glommers and pols — learn the mungo lingo
of the pay station and pie-card mission and play
footsy with the do-gooders.
                    Like Malletini —
he almost made me see straight, wanted me to love
mankind more than a man,

and I must say I did fall for them, naturally not quite all
at once but pretty many had this thing in common,
some sort of eye problem.
                    First there was Cross-Eyed Willy,
then Bad Eye, Goggles, and One-Eyed Jim.
Then Sir Thousand Loves — my name for him —
with his pale fragile pout and very *personal* eyes
and he was always going on and coming on — your all-
time word-fuck, if you please.
These eye-freaks, though, I had to hand it to them.
They usually took off their shoes.
                    Poor Malletini —
my best vision misses the far sight of him.

So it's back to the trains, and good to get back,
back to the bo garden, pro-le-beau ambish,
the voice of the road, hum of secret works, the whiz
and the whiffletree. As the likes of me has got to jump
some varnish, hotshot, dangler — don't matter which.
I know the ways of the roofer and the fox.
I like the push and pull together, being a sister,
blind baggage, feeling forever. . . .
I'd rather count ties, even grease the tracks, than wait
in the rat stand with a proper ticket and
your humdrum man.

So, Baby Dear, my one-shot stowaway, wherever you are
be there and please, go as you please.
The transient woman, from pull ear to push daisies,
takes a bitter-syrupy savvy for all her trouble,
but still . . . in all my lives I've had no true
tragedies to speak of, just your single-sigh
one-and-only-one . . . That hurts.
Baby Dear, all women are transients — born and raised
to try to be and to find — forgive me —
you just can't be any more than the only one we are.

$\mathcal{F}$ROM THE OPUS OF WILHELMINA SCROWD: WILHELMINA'S SUITE

1. Overture

Where *have* you been, Sweetums? I can't tell you
how many eleventh hours it seems Wilhelmina's been
waiting on you and hot to slobber her bibful,
freshing up the flashbacks, mugging some lines
for your spread, blowing my bubbles to the breeze . . .
Oh, yeah, the rubberneckers give me *that* look, you know . . .
As I say, the world's my waiting room . . . but wait,
before I get carried away, I mean to stick to my story,
hand you down some tips from how I got the stroke and bore
to handle my times out on the inside. You get this down, now.
See, every day for me, it's a walls-or-no-walls proposition.

2. Allemande

Now, I know how to talk myself in from the rain —
like, when you're in some fell of a hex, you get frazzled
to where the squeak and wet scratch in your lungs
is like a nest of kittens tied in a sack . . . Or, say
you just get in a freak funk and go on the potluck scent
of punished soup, coming up loud in your mouth glands
like an expiring onion . . . Then, maybe the dim surrounds
of a charity get to seem less plagueful than the sharp lumps
of numbed-out gloom in your shoes or, sometimes, just
from exploring the four corners of your heart
like some goofball Columbus, you might get this notion
to put your back up against four walls at once.

Then, natch, you've got this cootie in your ear,
how the do-gooders like to lock you in and rub your brain,
what's left on the surface of it, raw as a fresh burn
with cross-kid hintimations, sin-mortality and bug-tests.
But then, other streetpoop has it how those Misery Coops are
o.k., sometimes copasettee, anchors to windward
when you're on your beam ends . . . sooo . . .
But still, you got to watch out. You can so easy disappear
after a bout of whirling around like a wind-up toy ballerina
with this key jammed in her back. It's been like this for me,
I'm sorry to say, and where I couldn't wake up so much
I'd just as soon slip through to na-pooh land.

3. *Rondo*

My first time in, I must say, I was innocent.
I had this bum hunch of somebody just taking out the key
and letting me lay me down to sleep. But instead,
they tied me to a chair and drowned me in Kwell
to off all the crawlies in my ears and hairs.
I'm noting the hole in a hanky, the ooze in the bowl,
the high smells of beer sunk deep in army-surplus wool,
and the smoky salt of a cloaked cleavage. I take in
the talking meat all around — it's mostly women, victims
of mink, moth-cut eyelashes from Love's Discount plus
vermouthy cologne — all that coy-elegant scapegoatishness,

liaison and shady lingo, in which I participate, dirt-dappled
as a skylight under a sun with its muzzle off. You can see it
this way — all a kissy-kissy bingo without cards or beans,
this mumble — rattle, scurry, and shush, like a solo body
trap-set, as I said before, playing to tempos that would like
to tear your foot off, if you'd only be dumb enough to let go . . .

Then they brought me needles and this yellow peril
shrimp of a headshrinker came with the glim
from his silver stick, and this mirror coiled round
a hole in the middle of his forehead, and somehow,
Dearheart, he siphoned all the light right out of my eyes.
I still, to this day, do not know what he did with it.
He didn't know any language, not even so much
as your regular American dog or rattlesnake could understand.
This, of course, was never in my plan. And a long time after,
I thought I would be grieving to death, and the key
still stuck between my shoulder blades. Well, I found out,
it's always going to be there, but you get used to it.
The trick is to turn it yourself.

4. *Gigue*

Just wait . . . I'm thinking how to give you the picture,
the big one . . . like, maybe you're doing this
connect-the-dots puzzle, but then the dots are all on the move,
say, like trained fleas gone nuts. Still, you'd be surprised
what can come of a long stare at any type skewage — seen or unseen —
that is, if you happen to be long on the knack of sitting tight,
which is one of the finest arts, in my book anyways,
and, not to brag, all things considered, I've got a natural talent.

Listen, it can be taught. So, there's no time wasted, Dearie,
and now you're here, and you've got your connections, why not
make me a talking head, eh? Expose me to the big ad freaks —
this is America, there's no lifestyle can't be sold, right?

The Product, Honey? It's Image — ME — pave star, consultant.
Make Wilhelmina big enough, you can do it, you can sell tickets
to the risk. People are paying to learn how to walk on hot coals.
See what I mean, Sweetie? There's angles, here, there's curves,
there's all the ways round the bends to my type expertise,
and we'll sell it creative, we'll sell it *aspirational*. We'll do
a book: *Help Your Self: Achieving the Avenues.* Or, get this:
Wilhelmina's Top Ten Subways to the Sublime. Come to think,
it's just what the Chip-a-Roo off the old Block Party gazpacho
dirt bike Krazy Glue Amaretto antique Austrian Taco
Monopoly Time just-short-of-true-sleaze Disco World,
for visionaries only, wants. Trust me. The story is this:
How I did the death and didn't die to do it. Yeah.

Look at the magic aspect, the saint aspect. We'll sell
the nothing-to-lose zero-stress (Type Z) temporary ownership
of zilch, like your solar energy. I'll do workshops,
private lessons. Open will get to be the in place to be,
rags the top-line wear off the rack, talk the ticket.
Wonder no more. Find out what you're missing. Learn to *be*
that Missing Person. They'll come to school with me,
wear my shoes out the door. Have entree to our Stoop-by-Night,
our up-to-date Dorado, Leona's come-uppance to come.
Anon, come home to yourself — alone, tough, nonelegant,
a better person, on the whole . . . but, to go back . . .

5. *Badinerie*

So now. Say you limp yourself in to one of these sanctum
sanctoriums for the grub and chummery. You've got the working
biffies and lavs in mind, sticks and feathers galore.
You suck up your sad coffee and make loose button eyes
at the come-on-put-down social jerker, her snobocrat jaw
all the time working like the metal spring of a clothespin
in search of the perfect all-wet pillowcase to corner
and line up in a hot breeze. You know, open and shut,

open and shut. So there you are. You try to keep up
an agreeable twist of the pan, that is, without getting the arf-arfs —
as all a mirthquake means to them is bughouse for sure.

For all I know, *you* may think like some of them do
in those stainless rat traps, that my loon-lingo, all this
mock crap-out chin-chin I so carefully cook up to give,
all toasty and toady, is just a simple matter of leakage
from where some screws dropped out of my brain pan long ago
from dry rot, went and left some chewed-up peepers in the hull.

So much do they know. I'm telling you, you better believe
I've got some cover on my wagon. What I do
is not the old hysteria nut-puree, you know, but just
the minimal slobby gossip games of their so-called
"depressive position" maybe. What I do, I lay on
the plush and let them write down the given
name of my weakness, and the date of my address.

So you sit, as I said, tight . . . in your croaker joint
or Hotel de Gink or whatever, glamorous as the deckle-edge
of a hangnail, flabbergasted most likely from the cold
gust of a cubicle, but trying not to show it. It's funny,
how they never give you credit for being able to read
upside-down, so you get inside their silence, where they write
"schizoid — contumacious," or (I like this one) "affect — willfully
perverse." That, my dear, is Balm Beach style, for dingaling.
I might go pattering away from Svengali to Rice-A-Roni, say,
and concentrate — go slow or fast, turn my key just enough
to keep their ears perked, my bum in a warm seat,
and my wreath-of-roses feet on the ground. That's when
it's going good, but I'm not saying it's your easy cake.
Then I usually get the lecture again, how easy it is to die
from having the wrong life like I do, and I'm thinking how
I might be obliviated sooner from their swift handfuls of sounders
to the gut. Oh, someday, I'd like to kick some fire
into those Sugar Plum Fairies, with their humbug smiles,

their mouths crammed alphabet alleys, each bare tooth saying
something different, the tongue sparking off against those tusks
with a hiss like a just-missed train smooching off down the tracks.

But I've got it down to an -ology now, if not an -ism:
to bunk the jitters and tinpottiness, help whoever's holding
my pie-ticket to sugar the manure. You just sit
simple, gaze at the melody, thumb up the per usual drop dead
conventionals, do doormat imitations, expect what you get.

6. Sarabande

So, my dear, another day, another dolor, but moving
right along, what I have to say . . . it's simply this
tricky matter of putting one day behind the other.
The first hundred years, they say, are the hardest . . .
So, good-bye, and welcome elsewhere . . . Add to that how
I, Wilhelmina, love the rumpled talk in the street air, all
ripped and begging to be rewoven, all those scandalous
sheets with prospects, gospels, threats, pure filthy angelic
entertainments, none better, my own self wrapped up
in this basic scratch and light, a lady-in-waiting.
A genuine calling it was, and is, to me: to be
gifted, go it blind into a walk of life (the conviction
born of eviction, don't you see?), in full career
on the stroll — it's got to be the stage of stages . . .
And now you here, the come-off of all my fat hunchings,
after these years of decking the worst traumas
of my nothing-doings and all along keeping the right
to be lousy and hungry if I want . . . all I've got
is this want of some notices, some press
to lay my life out flat in black and white, my brains
with a sharp spiffy crease to their rag. You bet,
I can carry the hotsy-totsy type, the all-cap spreadhead.
Give me tombstones, Honey, or put me in your Living section.

I'd make a super running story, with a hole in the sock
ending. Homes don't interest me, but I would like a lot
of house, Darling — who wouldn't? — so see if you can do me
up right and sincerely to my basic ways. An entrance,
walk-on with exits and — oh, it's mucko, for sure —
and exits pursued — but anyway, tell me,
what are daydreams for?

7. Minuet

Now, you . . . Well, so you can choose to go along
some of those tracks someday . . . picture the traumas
of the haunts where even your ghosts give up their ghosts, or
you can go to where the gumtious bums roast stray dogs
in the Square — if that's what you want, for solace or make-ado.
Or, you can just lay back and give the bloody wind a chance,
dreaming of a snooze with hot doctor's magic, or . . .
of pimps with silver pencils and two-tone shoes.
Or, you can walk and walk yourself silly into a trance
of pitch-palaver, like I do . . . 'til the loose
whispers start to go loud and nearly public . . . I guess
that's my own favorite of all . . . the heart's off-again,
on-again, off off media . . . but then, it's only one
of the many ways I know . . . to solve the silence. Now,
you can go ahead and print that, Precious, as all I know
to say. Or, as one of all the possible combinations.
Make me your conversation piece. Dine out on me.

I don't mind at all being an imaginary person. Do you?

Part Two $\mathcal{S}$ A I D & D O N E

Zeus said: "You wanted fire — why settle for less than the whole shebang?" Such was Zeus' original forgiveness.

— Pandora Mud

PORTRAIT OF THE ARTIST
AS A YOUNG BITCH

-elf: delf, elf, Guelph, pelf, self, shelf . . .
— *Random House Vest Pocket Rhyming Dictionary*

She owns such a sad little life.
She writes about it all the time.
She whines. She is no body's wife,
And she would make that rhyme.

Or else she's Queen of the Heroines:
"Some genius should write about me —
How curious, how scrupled my sins . . . "
(She sighs) " . . .what delicate irony

I'd like to provoke." She loves a man,
And she has left him, too.
She's apt to make fun, as much as she can,
Of the ruins she's capered through.

She studies the books on her shelves,
The ones she thinks might translate her
Wonder to order, yield slants on her selves,
Or morally tag her with words as obscure

And ashamed as her own. She pays
In hard-earned coin the market price
For sainthood: willful despair and disgrace.
She'd love to spend forty days in some nice

Hot desert: exile, mangling, hood.
"Let me go for broke, cracked belle
Of despair; let my halo ring wide
Of my dome, Saturnian ruffle."

She *listens* for unlikely rhymes, as if
a *skill* could mask *self* in *person,*
stealth rattle soft music from *coffin;*
sound tune bone to reason:

$$AS\ IF:$$
her epitaph.

ONE DESIGNING WOMEN: COCO CHANEL

I. *Imagine wearing something . . .*

> *A well-dressed woman is closest to being naked.* *

Imagine wearing something as if
you didn't. Imagine you could move as if
you did. Imagine dressing down to where
you start.
        It's not the body between the lines
in tact I hand you but the hands
that make and make the lines and let the body
move to move
               you — a woman dressed in myth —
made up and over and closest to being . . .

Done: *Integrity is mystery.*
                     If you will,
imagine the perfect dress, invisible
with emphasis, a skin that, ripped, won't bleed.

Imagine! wearing something that dies on you —
if I wear a flower it's an artificial one.

---

* The individual sonnet titles are things Chanel is reported to have said. The itali-
cized statements in the poems are also quotations from Chanel, or inventions in the
spirit of her words. My main source is the biography of Chanel by Edmonde
Charles-Roux, trans. Nancy Amphoux (New York: Knopf, 1975).

III. *To run away nowhere* . . .

To run away nowhere, that's what we need underneath it all.
— Pierre Reverdy

The holidays were boring at Valette,
that gorgeous imaginary convent where
my sister and I were pampered, scolded, taught
to sit like ladies balancing their tea-
cups on their knees . . .
                     Valette, if only I
had seen it — mass and naked stone, the rags
and filthy toenails, beards, sweat, beggary
under the untouchable elegance . . .
                     Valette . . .
nothing remains of it.
                     Only an Au-
bazine orphan could imagine it, and Friar
Etienne in tatters scooping the cesspool out,
his saint's life going unsainted, founding

Aubazine — too real place I can't name . . .
Spoiled brats, we couldn't wait to get home.

V. *I'd rather have a touch of the Invisible*
than roast mutton every day.

I don't design for corpulence or corpse
but for something burning in between the terms
of mask and meat.
                     How do I keep my figure?
A gardenia for breakfast, for dinner an orchid,
Then I measure.

Elegance is sacrifice
hidden, with lines cut naturally, loosened
gracefully
                    so you can sense what is
underneath it all — the working muscle —
you should be able
                        to see the thigh and everything

that goes . . . goes on. A woman must be able
to stoop and run, embrace and fly, be supple
as seaweed,
                dune subtle or dry thistle
tinged with what's taken in and not forgot and not
meant to be
                    seen: luxury —
outside and in.

VI. *A copy is love.*

Turning the uniforms of the 10th Light Horse
into red pajamas for the Ritz under siege,
light-fingering a lover's coats and jodhpurs
to mime the groom, to horse or bride, blasé,
ransacking Westminster's togs and tweeds
and sailing blazers, outfitting and out-
fashioning the rich with the stuff of underwear,
I spread my lover's predilections out
in the marketplace: I make them simple so
I can be copied. *I think more of the common
street than drawing room. A copy is
a tribute to creation* — my love making
free with appearances — let it be
multiplied with bogus pearls — like me.

XI. *For me, fashion is not amusing — it's something on the edge of suicide.*

Born under the lion like Nostradamus,
born at dusk, always sad at the close
of day, I've lived on a staircase and felt
the collection would never pass.

                        I've knelt
at the feet of mannequins and stars, my heart
in stitching time, life, lines . . . *It's craft, not art.*
With fashion — what woman would want to kill
herself for an image every spring and fall?

A woman should say yes, say I believe
in everything — I do: in freedom, work,
accident, distrust of taste, pale orch-
ids, pearls, the senses, my number five . . .

No, fashion is not a joke: on some it may be
devastating, but on me it's deadly.

XII. *It's anger that gets work done.*

It's thunder and instinct, a mouthful of pins,
the needle taste salt metal sweet

                              (a child
tastes this in screaming the anger of being
abandoned, her fist exalting her bloody nose) —
       it is to make them see
       how I see red.

Come nearer, Child. What woman would wear this rag?
Stand straight, head up. What a drowsy jade you are
today. Whim and trash. Your hair's a sight. No, I'm not
through, but one more sigh and you will be. Now walk.

Raise your arms. Lower them. Raise. Lower. Keep on,
keep walking, Dummy, so I can see you in that mirror.
Somnambulant ostrich. Cut it. More pins. Don't flinch at me.
I'm making you. That's right. Go on — cry. Christen it.
    . . . and I need a red scarf, here, at the throat
    of her heart.

XIII. *The future has a nose.*

> *A badly perfumed woman has no future.*
> — Paul Valéry

A perfume needs its own body to move,
but whale's belly, beaver's groin, and civet's tail
can make a monster no one would dream of
kissing. Gardenia can stifle heaven.
A woman . . .
            is a woman and should not smell
like anything else, an abstract . . .
                        The future
has a nose for essence. Valéry was right.

My secret: jasmine and the synthetic
tenacity of mystery, and my knack
to note:
        *when a magnolia begins
to rot it smells of mushrooms.* Give me
that and grass and humus, *the whiff that makes
you remember* and leads the future by
its nose, that leaves a wake.

XVII. *To run away nowhere...*

To run away nowhere...
— Pierre Reverdy

One sort of designer puts marks on paper
and that is an art; a fashion designer

uses scissors and pins on cloth and flesh and that

is a news item. My tongue is running on
as there are those that come to listen

thinking they can get a story out of what

I say. It's too late now. The circle's done
and everywhere the center's nowhere — Jeanne —

my maid — she finds me sleeping on my feet

naked in darkness fondling my nightmare,
scissors in hand and my nightgown on the floor

in shreds. It is my life, to divide and cut

to the heart in pieces I am shrinking running down
this way Ritz corridors in white pajamas nowhere

and nothing underneath but what dies on one.
Imagine wearing something — a scent, a flower ...

ALL ISADORA

for Naomi Lebowitz

> *Thus I want man and woman: the one fit for war, the other fit*
> *to give birth, but both fit to dance with head and limbs. And we*
> *should consider every day lost on which we have not danced at*
> *least once. And we should call every truth false which was not*
> *accompanied by at least one laugh.*
>
> — Friedrich Nietzsche, "On Virtue That Makes Small,"
> *Thus Spake Zarathustra**

I. *Always Moving*

Out of the sea under Aphrodite's star
Out of the orchestra of shadows and my soul's motor

> An art, a school, a baby . . . what more
> can you create?
> > I came to move as no one
> had ever moved before,
> > > then I moved as ten
> or twenty or fifty maidens at Zeus' altar

Out of the sea under Aphrodite's star
Out of the orchestra of shadows and my soul's motor

> One's childhood is always moving . . . not just
> to keep ahead

---

* All epigraphs are either from Nietzsche's *Thus Spake Zarathustra* or from the poems
of Walt Whitman. Isadora referred to these writers as her "dancing masters."

of cold and the rents and the ranting landlord,
or to keep afoot
of the revolutions of the world,
but to be the star, the flower, the prayer, the most
moving of all
as in that salty swell
and well my mother
Terpsichore taught me

Out of the sea under Aphrodite's star
Out of the orchestra of shadows and my soul's motor

One's childhood is for life.

III. *Opening in Budapest (1903)*

I am still virgin — to open in Budapest!
For thirty nights I am to dance
a revolutionary hymn in Budapest
and through the Blue Danube, my first big deal.

Goulash and heavy wine in Budapest,
Golden Tokay, ardent eyes and all . . .
I meet my Romeo in Budapest
with purple light in his licorice hair.

He plays his part for me in Budapest
or just outside, in a peasant's hut and then
he switches roles and baffles me in Budapest
opening just to close.
I swallow hard
a bushel of broken glass in Budapest —
my first — big deal — love's labors lost.

IV. *A Mixed Letter to Gordon Craig*

> *Was somebody asking to see the soul?*
> — Walt Whitman, *Starting from Paumanok*

Dear Growly Tiger,

          The days here glide
by like gondolas but between the bills
and mosquitoes
          and you and me life's not so *gai.*
    A funny made toy — me — I'm tired
to tatters — been doing some Big Magic
practicing and got some Big Magic Pains
for thanks —
          been tearing up letters too — me
    to you — misabel, affreuse — Nope — love and work
don't mix.
          Some times I dance 'til even my soul
perspires — then Topsy's all electrics and full
of wake-ups — then nerves and devils —
    'stonishing!
Schmerzen and powders — nothing
          works — meanwhile
I'd better go to America and find me
a millionaire.
        Love meyou darling —
            Your Topsy

VIII. *Opera Comique*

Champagne and flattery —
the pagan body — Lethe —
Zarathustra — all — ravishing me

not only
in the blood-lit grotto
    & grail goblet measures
    of Wagner's genius . . .
    temples/times/tempos . . .
but every place I go . . .

    The Singer-Man called Paris
    called me Isis
    & sailed me away & not nine stitches
    too soon as
    he left me
knowing love might be

a pastime as well as a tragedy.

IX. *Turning Backward*

It was not as if I was not prepared for the worst.
    But who pays real attention to
the odd stare of a fortune-teller
as she tallies the children in the web
of your loose fist?
           Who dreams the nightmare
will bolt home to your stable to stay? Who trusts
the attack of vision? *Little white coffins in a row*
in the snow, out of nowhere.
           I should have known.
           I should have known.

I tucked my two angels into the back seat
of their limousine. Kissed Deirdre through the glass.
Little Patrick danced, tipped Nurse Sims' hat

over her eyes and the motor began and the wheels
began to turn to take them away toward the bank
of the Seine. The wheels . . .

        turn backward then.
        Turn backward then.

X. *No Show No Rainchecks*

Creation — that is the great redemption from suffering. . . .
Indeed, there must be much bitter dying in your life, you
creators. . . . To be the child who is newly born, the creator
must also want to be the mother who gives birth.
        — Nietzsche, "Upon the Blessed Isles"

All ready to go on — the stage set
with the grayblue fluent curtains.
Overcome, my star dancers fall down . . .
           Over them
the curtain eddies slightly — then quiet.

Meanwhile, the audience can hold its breath, sit tight
only so long.
      A ripple?
          The light man steps down
to regret — the stars will not appear tonight.
Money will be refunded.
        I can't go on.

The sound a woman utters at the moment
of childbirth is the same — returning the flesh
of my flesh to its terrible perfection
I wanted to console everyone —

              as at the moment
of death.
        I fall into the large arms of Duse —
no greater tragedienne.
        Can we go on?

XI. The Red Sails before Sunset

> *Did we think victory great?*
> *So it is — but now it seems to me, when*
> * it cannot be help'd, that defeat is great,*
> *And that death and dismay are great.*
> > — Whitman, "To a Foil'd European Revolutionaire"

The money gone again, I give my last
bows at the raving Bolshoi, say good-bye
to the school that was always less than I
dreamed and begged for.
> Three years of dust

brushed from the hatbox lid, I open it,
but not all the dark flies out; a tatter
stays, twitches, scurries — and before
I know what I am doing — in a fright — my heart
trembles to smash — its web snaps.
> I kill it.

Now think: that spider was born inside
here, lived lightless — no inkling of it — and then
by this hand — something it had never known
floods its world — revelation — I open
a place beyond darkness. The shoe is in
my hand.
> *Revelation and the end coincide.*

XIII. Russia: Coming and Going

> *Alas, where shall I climb now, with my longing?*
> > — Nietzsche, "On the Land of Education"

Arriving — Narva — I couldn't wait to begin
my new life. I got out my gramophone
on the station platform, danced for a throng
of peasant kids. Then I had them dance along.
But no one met me in Petrograd. No money.
When they gave me children there were only forty.

I'd asked for a thousand at least — to start.
All in little red tunics, each dancing her part
to the Internationale, to the Revolutionary
Spirit of the dance itself. . . . It was not to be.
I was a Big Wheel. But cold, hungry. Needed oil.
They told me to sell myself to support my school.
I did. From West to East: Come full circle.
Three years we scraped along. I went on tour
in and out of the Soviet State, but never
managed to save as much as I gave away.

My last time out — in Tashkent — I thought I'd die.
Without a kopeck, without a cup of tea,
creaking from catastrophe to catastrophe
(there is no transportation for me — even
the soul's — that doesn't trap me or break down).
At last my car fell in two between nowhere
and nowhere; my curtains mildewed en route; my hair
turned white — no henna shampoo; completely broke
and kaput. Even my last flight out didn't lack
emergency. And there beside the damaged plane
I gave some peasant kids an impromptu lesson
to the wheeze of an accordion — the Internationale
of course, as I'd arranged it, in a spiral —
just once more, with feeling: *Come, full circle.*

XVII. *Reviving a Cuban Bacchanal: A Dancing Lesson*

> *After all not to create only, or found only,*
> *But to bring perhaps from afar what is already founded,*
> *To give it our own identity, average, limitless, free.*
> — Whitman, "Song of the Exposition"

O it's all very rum rum rum so rum . . .
To be on your toes
        does not mean you have to break
metatarsals and laws of gravity.

I believe in the intelligence of the human foot.
I worship in the natural arch of the human foot.
I bless my unbroken toes, the little with the large,
the evolution of them.

O it's all very rum rum rum so rum . . .
That peculiar is eternal
                    does not mean you have to break
your heart to deviate.

I believe in the solar plexus that lets me
dance Christ on Calvary to a Cuban tango, lets me
turn the cancan into my Mater Dolorosa, lets me
dance the loony swine into the sea.

    I believe in all of me. The chorus of tragedy.
    I've never once danced a solo.
    Don't let me
    down.

To be on your toes
strictly naturally strictly
                    does not mean you have to break
to change as you choose.

O it's all very rum rum rum so rum
to change as you choose
to abandon the body for rhythm
naturally, to be on your toes.

XVIII. Writing My Life

My brothers, one knows a little too much about everybody.
— Nietzsche, "On the Pitying"

My Life, my foot! The publisher says put it
on the front burner, stir, stir, stir — taste
for spice. If not enough add little bits —
minced apocrypha. Taste? Debatable. Haste.

Here's one bit that's not — but might be — hot:

It happened in my Leningrad honeymoon suite.
Years after the Event. My ungainly poet
took some ink from his left wrist vein and wrote
"Good-bye. Neither death nor life is anything
new," and hanged himself. Is that what you want?

My Life, my eye! I saw America dancing
once. Now . . . it seems irrelevant.

Walt, old scribe of my eyes, where are you?
Nietzsche, amanuensis to my feet . . . you too?

XX. Last Words with Mary Desti (September 14, 1927, Nice)

*O you visions and apparitions of my youth! O all you glances of
love, you divine moments! How quickly you died. . . .*
— Nietzsche, "The Tomb Song"

Remember, Mary, how the last time in Paris —
Schubert's *Ave Maria* — how I danced the arms
alone, cradling nothing?
                              Art has climaxes;
life only anticlimaxes, alarms.

Phooey. Fourteen years. I can't get them out of
my mind. Children.

I wanted to console everyone
the day they drowned.

My school . . .

Remember the Love-
Death of Isolde? The Funeral March of Chopin?

My glories.

Lay me down in the purple cloak.

But how nice Nice is now I've got my eye on
that Bugatti, its driver . . . What a joke!
We're broke.

Put "Blackbird" on the gramophone,
will you?

Pack up all my cares and woe,
Here I go, singing low,
Bye, Bye Blackbird.
Where somebody waits for me,
Sugar's sweet, so is he . . .
So make my bed and light the light,
I'll be home late tonight,
Blackbird, Bye, Bye.

I'll dance to that! A closed car
is not my style.

Where's my red shawl?

He's here.

We're off! Adieu, mes amis, je vais a ma gloire!

THE PLAYMATE:
OPHELIA BACKSTAGED

for Kenneth Burke

> *My history, my love,*
> *Is but a choice of speech.*
> — W. H. Auden

So here I sit, friends, not a stitch on,
no time to lose, not a word to say;
again, with the play not over yet
again, in fact, the play barely begun.
Who could blame an ordinary Ophelia
for having had it up to here with a script
not likely to change, or instruct from its end.
Who could blame an Ophelia like me
for hating her greasy face,
her messy wardrobe and cracked mirror, her
dabbling between flats and acts and wobbly wings,
with S. M. Daddy and Angel and Gaffer and every other
angry and knocking *oh hurry hurry up you silly cow hurry*
up only a minute to go as if I didn't know
how to put something on in time.

Night after night after night
the identical ominous fuss ripples through
my floorboard's splinters and my dressing room's
slammed door. And I forget where we are.
Ready for this stupid sprigged pelisse
with seamy syntax drooped down to my toes?
The indigo linen wrinkling so elegantly
around my silences? Or how about this cloak
that swished so much like wit once round

my heroine stuff and strut and now
all these beauties hang round my neck much more
like the suspended sentences shoplifters angle for.

KNOCK knock   knock knock knock KNOCK

Here's a gown for drowning in. What a joke!
I've grown far too fat for it,
never mind how sweetly my once trim torso's lines
lay memorized in its tucks and darts
like love letters, stiff cross-stitched ghosts.
Our Stage Manic Cur scuffs and barks, huffs off.
Oh what I wouldn't give
for a pair of pajamas with feet in them,
so easy to slip into, wriggle out of
in time to get into the more tacky sleeves,
and skin-pinching dickies all itchy inside
with emergency mendings bright as those empty
elm stumps raddle-patched with witches' butter.
I hear blackbirds bathing in melted snow.
And Lady Madness ever, ever so timely with her props,
sends me her howling lapdog on a leash,
and such lovely bouquets — cattails, kumquats,
flabby owl feathers, moonseed and lichen.
Lady M. is the stage manager's good good friend.
I hear you, both, Bitch! You Bastards!
All that fuss.   All that fuss.

Yet the fuss seems hardly over love as much as over
being, being over, and so very out of it
as usual I prepare to go down
with my bated breath intact,
to be dulcet as any ingenue all of a piece
baiting her trap, his traipsing innocence.

My debut, each night, is part trick part script;
each night I step out and center pretending
to have a prayer, to have a prayer for you,
sweet wives, putting off the acts of your lives.

After the "Who's there?" there's no stopping.
But for just a moment, to be sorting out
my garland and train of cross-stitched pansies,
those fine lines Hamlet so thrills to
step on. Night after night, my yakky father
falls down again dissolved in patter
like salt in drizzle and I come into my own
small rain of syllables
in good time arranging the snowdrops, nettles,
long purples hand-picked to beguile the breezes
Pater's been sending to sail me down
the river at last rushing song
into rushed song . . .

where I will be married at last again to nothing
but words, sweet lays in the last thin airs
I put on with my pearl choker and skew of leaves:
bindweed, dodder, loosestrife,
stems of fox grape, asphodel, rue.
Here and here, I button them, tiny carnations,
wee purses of silence . . . I'll do,
                              and I do, I do,
I do become the word's wife
before I can be widowed in those weeds,
once again, I do put on
the act of my life.

I call it my diamond solitaire,
Although it's emerald as grass
(Is that why you stare?)
And the object is to amass

As many points as I can.
The points on the diamond are marked
With chalk and bags of sand
Against the green. I am marked

By a madness of numbers.
I play nine parts
And lead nine lives. I'm limber;
I live by short stops, false starts,

And crowds of angels: base men,
Outfielders, catchers, pitchers, umpires . . .
Of course, it's all in my mind —
I play in a league of desires.

Why are you so blank? It's as if you
Had never seen a game like this before.
It's a kind of swell melodrama. Hiss. Boo.
Cheer. I'm going to try it once more.

See how I run circles around this square,
The object being to get home,
Where home, as if I could care,
Is that trampled splotch I started from.

But how can I teach you anything?
Love me, love me. That's my only game.
I'll be your living doll. I'll sing
And I'll dance. I will waste no shame.

I call it my diamond solitaire,
Or my cold emerald merry-go-round.
I plan to outgrow myself, sick of the fair
I've run into the earth's fair grounds.

$\mathcal{T}$HE TERRIBLE MEMORY
OF LIZZIE BORDEN*

Remembering August 4, 1892

I was in the yard. I heard a groan.
I came in and found Father —

                    I found him
stabbed or something —   Go, get Doctor Bowen,
Maggie, hurry.

                    Mrs. Churchill, please come
over —   Someone has killed Father — I
came in and found him — in the sitting room —
don't look —

                    There is his eye it's awful — eye
split right in two and hanging — running from
his cheek.

                    And Mrs. Borden must be out
because she said that somebody was sick
this morning and she said she had a note —
but wait — I think I heard her —

                    Better look —

No — I don't want — I want to be — alone.
                    Now
who could have done   this thing?
                    He's dead —   and how —

---

* On August 4, 1892, Lizzie Borden's father and stepmother died of multiple ax wounds, in their own home. Lizzie was at home that morning, and rushed to report her discovery of Mr. Borden's mangled, still warm, corpse. Before and after Lizzie's arrest, a week later, she was repeatedly asked one question: "Where were you at the time?" Her reiteration of unfathomable alibis indicate pretty clearly that, murderess or not, Lizzie Borden had a terrible memory.

Remembering Answering

who is not going to ask me that again.

I was out. I was in the loft. I went to look
for some tin to fix my screen. I think it took
half an hour or less. The door was open.
I heard a scraping noise and I came back
and there was Father . . .
                                . . . early — not yet noon —
and he was dead I helped him to lie down
and went out . . .
                              I heard a scraping in the lock
and Maggie let him in. I was coming down
the stairs. He was mad because his key stuck.
I calmed him. Maggie was up in her attic.
We talked some. He asked where is Mrs. Borden.
She's gone   she had to go   some one   was sick
he was   asleep   I went   out and then   came back.
who is not going   to answer that   again

Remembering My Morning

I might have been down cellar or in my room
washing up or basting a loop on the dress
I had to change into or putting a stick on the fire
to heat the flats to iron the sprinkled stuff . . .
I do not do things quickly.
                              It took me

by surprise —

                              half an hour to eat three pears

in the barn loft, then look for lead to make
sinkers for some fishing lines

                                    I haven't got
yet isn't it odd

                              I didn't hear the crash
that lard pail must have made when she fell down
and yet I hear the Quequechan that runs
so crazy underground and through the heart
of Fall River and drives the thumping looms
to cloth and cash in

                              torrents . . . and I laugh

Remembering Him Coming Back

at the top of the stairs. Yes, that was quite out
of character — I'm truly sorry — See I am
crying — what you've got to believe if you can. . . .
Me ?   Now?

                        Did I know how to use a hatchet?
Hardly. But neither did that idiot
who mangled them,   though. . . . There's no certainty
where I am then.

                        Now then . . . precisely?
here and there.

                        It's kind of hard to split
hairs with an ax. I'm trying to manage but
my head is splitting.

                        Just leave me alone.
I am Someone . . .

                        and someone killed . . .

                                          a Borden
No skeleton but that in the closet

of my own flesh and blood I am afraid.
Could they have committed double suicide?

Remembering Is Difficult Days Running Together

I was out.
I mean in the barn.
I had some pears.
Last night too.

I mean I was out back.
It is so hot in the house.
Everybody is sick.
I went to see Alice

. . . and I told her
one was going to do some-
something awful — we were
dispensing poison

about the poison some-
thing — I could feel it
sure a doom-
to the family — that.

It wasn't just
this rotten heat
to poison us. . . .
somebody outside

old mutton on the stove,
the milk in our blood
had to be the work of
Father's . . . misunderstood. . . .

Enemies — nobodies —
Father was *somebody*.

enemies —
they had to do it.

Remembering Things

Now I believe in things and all the things —
slop pail, stepmother, feather duster, flats
for ironing, Maggie's mop, mysterious note,
cookies, Father's papers, sticks in the fire,
needle and thread, et cetera. . . . I say
you can find, you *should* be able to find.

But where I was, and when, I just can't say.
I swear the pears were dropping one by one.

I never said anything about an ax
handle. I said I put a stick in the fire.
I never said I didn't burn a dress —
I said it was too filthy to wear anymore.

I swear I went in and out and out and in.
I swear the pears were dropping one by one.

Remembering Being Arrested (August 11, 1892)

Is that question meant to mix me up?
Because I am mixed up enough by now.
Why ask me then? Let's get it over with.

You have searched this place and every place
you found me out you found me out of it.

What you take me for, I can't believe
in but take me in since
                              I've always wanted
to be a center of attraction where

as now maybe I am:
                              a self-made orphan
appealing to all types —
                              the Bloomer Girls,
my sidekick clerics, ladies' mags, inkpots,
crackpots, pressed and unpressed —
                              Look for me
in a witness box, barn box, belly box, jury
box of your own —
                              accord won't find me
                              guilty.

Remembering My Trial (June 5, 1893)

They line the streets. They make me a carnival,
a teletype to the world, a scoop of ice
cream. Their tongues hang out, and how
they love the melt of me when Mr. Jennings

speaks of my baby fingers twisted in
my father's whitening hair — my little gold
ring on his little finger — the story of
the year the public curiosity,

the private one — the two of them — laid out
after a meal that would make anybody
drop — the Extra sheets turn yellow — in
an hour — they're hungry again for gush

and grue — the courtroom's filled with flowers and hacks
echo back and forth — to each what each likes
best.
      to be sure to be sure to
                  be there.

Remembering to Be a Legend

and everywhere at once, the whole world waiting.
I am conceived — a murderess — and spend
nine months locked in — and just for this — to be
reborn a martyr, reborn an orphan — born

again — a miracle. I have to take it,
my life in my hands and tiptoe through the door . . .

to be Lisbeth of Maplecroft nowhere inside;
to see Boston, and meet the lovely Nance O'Neil,
to hog all her tragic parts I'd like to play . . .

midwiving meanwhile the children's rude outspoken
chants

        that when I saw what I had done —
toward undoing

        the verdict

          I could go on.

To make a dragon move
(From the Diary of an Anorexic)

It would have starved a gnat
To live so small as I —
And yet I was a living Child —
With food's necessity

Upon me like a Claw
I could no more remove
Than I could coax a leech away —
Or make a Dragon — move —

— Emily Dickinson

I have rules and plenty. Some things I don't touch.
I'm king of my body now. Who needs a mother —
a food machine, those miles and miles of guts?
Once upon a time, I confess, I was fat —
gross. Gross belly, gross ass, no bones
showing at all. Now I say, "No, thank you," a person
in my own right, and no poor loser. I smile
at her plate of brownies. "Make it disappear,"

she used to say. "Join the clean plate club." I disappear
into my room where I have forbidden her to touch
anything. I was a first-grade princess once. I smile
to think how those chubby pinks used to please my mother.
And now that I am, Dear Diary, a sort of magical person,
she can't see. My rules. Even here I don't pour out my guts.
Rules. The writing's slow, but like picking a bone,
satisfying, and it doesn't make you fat.

Like, I mean, what would *I* want with a fat
diary! Ha Ha! But I don't want you to disappear
either. It's tricky. "Form in a poem is like the bones
in a body," my teacher says. (I wish he wouldn't touch
me — ugh! — he has B.O. And if I had the guts

89

I'd send him a memo about it, and about his smile.
Sucking the chalk like he does, he's like a person
with leprosy.) I'm *too* sensitive, so says Mother.

She thinks Mr. Crapsie's Valentino. If my so-called mother
is getting it on with him behind my back . . . That fat
cow! What would he see in her? Maybe he likes a person
to have boobs like shivery Jell-O. Does he want to disappear
between thighs like tapioca? His chalky smile
would put some frosting on her Iced Raspberry, his "bone"
(another word for IT, Sue said) stick in her gut,
maybe, bitten right off! Now why did I have to touch

on that gross theme again, I meant only to touch
on "thoughts too deep for tears," *and not my mother.*
That Immortality thing, now — I just have a gut
reaction to poems like that — no "verbal fat"
in poems like that, or in "the foul rag and bone
shop of the heart." My God! How does a person
learn to write like that? Like they just open to smile
and heavy words come out. Like, I just *disappear*

beside that stuff. I guess that's what I want: to disappear.
That's pretty much what the doctor said, touching
me with his icy stethoscope, prying apart my smile
with that dry popsicle stick, and he said it to Mother.
And now all *she* says is "What kind of crazy person
would starve herself to death?" There I am, my gut
flipflopping at the smell of hot bread, my bone
marrow turning to hot mud as she eases the fat

glistening duck out of the microwave, the fat
swimming with sweet orange. I wish it would disappear,
that I . . . If I could just let myself suck a bone —
do bones have calories? — I wouldn't need to touch

a bite of anything else. I am so empty. My gut
must be loopy-thin. Spaghetti. I chew on my smile.
Is lip skin fattening? I know Hunger as a person
inside me, half-toad, half-dwarf. I try to mother

him: I rock and rock and rock him to sleep like a mother
doing sit-ups. He leans his gargoyle head against the fat
pillow of my heart. But awake he raves, a crazy person,
turned on by my perpetual motion, by the disappearing
tricks of my body; his shaken fist tickles drool to my smile.
He nibbles my vagus nerve for attention. Behind the bone
cage of my chest, he is bad enough. He's worse in my gut
where his stamped foot means binge and puke. *Don't touch*

me, Hunger, Mother . . . Don't you gut my brain.
Bones are my sovereigns now, I can touch them here and here.
I am a pure person, magic, revealed as I disappear
into my final fat-free smile, where there is no pain.

THE PASSIONS
OF RAHEL VARNHAGEN

A Certain Freedom of Speech

*Lying is lovely if we choose it, and is an important component of
our freedom.* *

Don't tell me a flirt from the *Judengasse*
can't entertain a prince or hack in style.
Tell me what the fortune-teller said
last Thursday about you-know-who (more or less).

Don't tell me everything is so . . . indefinite,
or ask me if it's possible to love.
Tell me about the baron who had to sell
his two gold teeth to a Jew, and this-and-that.

Tell me your imaginary life
in all its detail; tell me about your passion
for strawberries or cats. Tell me another
fairy tale — thank God for them — and if

there's time, let's compare notes on suffering
(where facts matter less than a manner of speaking).

---

* All epigraphs, statements by Rahel Varnhagen, come from Hannah Arendt,
Rahel Varnhagen: The Life of a Jewish Woman, trans. Richard and Clara Win-
ston (New York: Harcourt Brace Jovanovich, 1974). The entire poem appears
in *In Light of Genius* (Philadelphia: Jewish Publication Society, 1981).

Pretending

Only galley slaves know each other.

Gossip is sweaty work. One doesn't chat
all afternoon to find out what life is like.

Under the lace and golden watch chains we're
straining to keep the secrets dressed, to fake
intimate infinities . . . and forget.

Today let's play we're galley slaves, all oars
put in one direction — against the wind
against the seas, against the circular

nature of nature. Is it because we've sinned
we're chained to each other and to the drift
of tyrannies no one can understand?

It's no use, pretending. We can't undress or lift
one finger to feel another's bare survival.

We belong with no one, no fast fellow-craft.

Viewing the Body

Our history is nothing but the history of our illness.

I'd rather wear a paper crown in bedlam
than give up grief — my best possession — proof
of having had.

Still, I suppose I am
ashamed of being inconsolable;
to be healed is harder than to heal.

I scavenge in others' losses, nurse others' fears.
My soul's half junkyard, half a hospital.
Beyond repair, beyond repair — I'm happy.

I finger the central scar by which we know
we were connected, are. This thing is dead.

Ashamed, one asks, should a corpse be viewed or not?

What choice is there? Cryptic is cryptic. Say:
"Fortuity is confusion's favorite toy."
Then gobble cakes and dance in your paper hat.

A Changed Person

I could not have done anything differently.

Forgetting — my favorite of life forces —
makes me fear reiteration less
where we begin and end, begin and end:
             a name can be a blessing or a curse.

Identities in deshabille, we think
we have a choice. We do. A drop of water,
mumbo-jumbo, a wedding ring, and Rahel
steps out:
             Antonie Friederike Robert Varnhagen von Ense.

Goethe once called on a person of that name.
I wasn't dressed. I fastened on my black
work skirt. I shook. I shook his hand. The chosen

one can't ask the center of the universe
to wait.
      When the great man left I changed to white
with lace.
            I had a rite to celebrate.

Too True a Reflection

> *In short, as if I stood before a temple of magic — for reality
> receded before my soul that was still not empty of life — a temple
> I can already see swaying; its collapse is certain and it will
> inevitably come down on me and everyone else.*

Deja vu et deja entendu,
a person can look outside history, past
the dreams, the lies, the theories and the true
transcendentalia of gossip.
                    At last
Cassandra sees that love has nothing to do
with what's real, save to grind tense present tenses
and present pain to the point of breaking through.

My pain is public knowledge. Romances
are no antidote for too much too true
reflecting.
              Cassandra with her presence
of mind plus dislocation had a clue
to chaos, intimacy with the blind
moment of losing, love.
                  *It's true
I see because I simply do not see*

how to be anything but glass, dark back
to the wall, dispensing smiles, feeling them . . . crack.

All Excluding

At my "tea table," I sit with nothing but my dictionaries.

How do you do and how do you define
a "trifle"? Pastry? Sex? Destiny?

No one calls here anymore. The fashion
is for titles, blue eyes, flag-waving, money . . .

Women, Philistines, Frenchmen, Jews — all are
suspect and/or excluded. I look up
"Philistine." Yes, I suppose I am. I hear
you're counted French — here, have another cup —

merci merci — if ever Napoleon was
your hero. Yes, still is. The best people
are the best people. That has been, and is,
my only attitude toward war. A trifle

stale, a trifle wasted, a life that trifles
with life itself . . . how many lay lonely tables?

Beau Monde

*How loathsome it is always having to establish one's identity
first. That alone is enough to make it so repulsive to be a Jew.*

Abroad I'm from Berlin, but in Berlin
I'm from the *Judengasse*. At home I am
my history's destiny. In Prague I am

what I am: an exile *par excellence.*

Varnhagen shows me there are ways to win
tickets to *bon ton* and glitter. One who is
adept at vogue and vagueness, letters and liaison,
can mingle at Teplitz with the arty bunch.

Now: married, baptized, renamed, I've arrived
at the masquerade, to stand on what's beneath
me now, that simply can't, can't, can't, can't simply be.

I'm from Berlin, the *Judengasse*, planet Earth.

Don't get me wrong — I'm grateful for a crown,
even if I have to wear it upside-down.

Before and After

> *When I am dead rescue the image of my soul.*

My heart is sore from the uneven chafe
of bliss — the itemless and timeless stroke
that excludes history. That's never enough
to counteract a life. That's pure bad luck.

I wonder what the image of my soul
might be —
            a constantly draining cup of tea,
a gem of the sort my father used to sell,
a bird house taken over by warring squirrels,
a fist full of fingers everything slips through . . .

It all runs down: just take a minute, multi-
ply it, waste it. I've done what I can do
to reassure those who come to tea, to grief,
to chatter or to nothing.
                        Is there life
after death they ask.   You bet.
                        I'm living it.

# AFTER ALL

I remember that I am falling
That I am the reason
And that my words are the garment of what I shall never be
Like the tucked sleeve of a one-armed boy
　　　　　— W. S. Merwin, "When You Go Away," *The Lice*

This will only hurt a little. We promise.
It's only your left foot, Sweetheart.
We need it. So many people are going hungry.
Until now you've had everything.
Now all we're asking you for is your foot.
That's all.

. . .

There.
It's over. You can begin saying it.
It's the only way.
Say it: *foot.*
foot   foot   foot   foot
That will be your medicine:
say it over and over again.

. . .

Well, well. Still here we see.
The boys are still talking about your fine foot, Dearie.
There has been nothing like it since.
And now we find you are superb with those new toes.
That is not empty flattery.
It's marvelous what concentration does,
isn't it? Don't look so scared.
We just had to come back for the left leg.

Easy, easy now. After all,
people just go on and on, you know,
having to be fed.

That wasn't so bad now, was it?
Those legs of yours have never been so fine.
Pick them out of any magazine,
they're yours. They're sound.
And as soon as you really feel what you say,
why, you'll be on your way.

. . .

We can see you're glad to see us again.
This won't take long — they're rather thin —
and soon your words should be arms enough
to hold *your* lovers in.

. . .

My head or my *head?*
I wasn't awake somehow
when they lifted the torso,
the breasts, the delicate shoulder blades . . .
but they must have noticed how those needed
to be raised

and I know they will come back to me
and I am so very glad
they have me to speak
my body, to exist
after all
I have been chosen for this
to feed this body
to the world, the body
politic, increasingly
to be chosen
and I am glad, glad . . .

who needs these eyes ears bones shell
and empty sockets when all
is so said
and done

my head   head   head   head   head
addressed to the world at last
and dressed with light
that bandage that binds the air
like sleep as I knew it would

and I am whole
I am good   I am good   I am good
I am very good.

Part Three $\mathcal{S}$ EEING THROUGH

And together we laughed between ourselves,
beside ourselves, inside ourselves.
There we were, ready to hold our own,
men coming to their conclusions alone.

— Sarai Abramsfrau

CASSANDRA

O apple-man, Apollo, your parched glance
appalls me. Did I say I'd lie with you
in exchange for the gift of gab?
                            No chance.
Your serpent licked my sleeping ear, it's true.

I saw enormity. I couldn't lie,
new-sighted and entangling as I was,
already big with portent, augury,
big with the gist and pith of your pythoness.

You made me kiss you —
                            spit into my mouth
snake-quick as wit, regret —
                            the taint of sham:
my woman's pain — unbearable —
                                    bearing truth
to men who put me down,
                            tell Troy I am
insane.

Troy burns. Now Agamemmon's blood . . .
I see —
            beyond belief — too soon,
                            too late — too bad.

BELLE STARR:
THE BANDIT QUEEN REMEMBERS

for Robert Taylor

beginnin a letter for my daughter, 1888

It's quieter'n a wood pussy walkin on the moonlight
at Younger's Bend without you Pearl
and your poor dumb brother run out as I took the quirt to him
pretty good for him riskin bein reduced to a cottonwood blossom
and after all his leather-bodied mother
has done by way of caution. But now that's enough
about Eddie, nothin but a hopeless son of that hopeless
guy Jim Reed. You now, my Pearl,
you are the daughter of Cole Younger who was and is
even if he is locked up in Stillwater
one of the legends we couldn't live without, and me.
Sometimes I reckon you are forgettin
just who you are and just who you are supposed to be.
Pearl Younger there ain't a single other soul
I ever had any hopes for save for yours. I gave you
a name to live up to and gave you plenty
lessons in how to be a lady and lessons how not to
serve out your time as some common
brainless calico. Now I don't know what you figure
you are doin with that bastard baby
of yours runnin away from home but you had just better
think again, my Pearl, and remember
just where you come from and say over your mother's name
and ponder how she's come to live with that.

a note to attach to that newspaper hooey

Pearl, Baby, there's just no tellin
what those tinhorn medicine tongues augurin
in the Police Gazette will cook up concernin
yours truly or the "Bandit Queen"
as one fop has kindly christened me.
I guess I'd be bored as a geldin in green-up time
if they didn't lift a pen to take a squirt at me
seein how much they muck about to enhance
Jesse and Frank and them other "dangerous" boys
I can wrap right around my pinkie easy
as a cowhand bindin the feet of a split tongue dogie.
But ever since the hangin judge
sent me and Sam Starr up to Pandemonium to weave
cane chair bottoms and split rock it's only Sam
that's had to go on the dodge
and my part's mostly gossip.
You don't have to believe your old Ma
is straighter 'n a wagon tongue, mind you,
but here I am aiming for mostly true
chin music to remind you, Pearl, that
even if I'm full of fool's words
it's not fool's gold I'm ever huntin for
and the heart in my aim is honester
than your Texas butter that is mostly lard.

remindin her how it wasn't easy even then

Fatman Parker ain't the only judge in my life.
Your grandpa was called "Judge" back in Carthage, Missouri,
where he kept sweet liquors, a civilized kitchen and wife.
        I used to dream. . . .
an Osage warrior might anytime crash our zigzag and steal
me away, first scalpin the "Judge" and Ma.
        Then I'd leave the Female Academy
to be a real bushwhacker, not just my brother's last
resort for scout. I'd smile and wink and spy my way
right into the Yankee ranks and leave them wonderin how
as they died. The closest I ever got to that — listen — I
know I've told it a million times, but Pearl, it's different now
you're grown with a woman's understandin of your own:

When I was scoutin and nosed out how the Jayhawk Yankees
were goin to drygulch my best brother Bud for his blood
revenges, and they caught me and ran me in to Judge Ritchery's,
I didn't just charm the lot by poundin out a gallopade
on his piano. I gave that burblin monster
just what he asked for in his privatest chambers.

You might say that was the day my spirit put my body on
ice, thin ice, like the November slick on a pond
you see your face skim over as you're fallin in.

a word about power plus a second thought

Just because I knew my power as a woman, Pearl,
I didn't stop with that. Even before Bud was chilled
I learned to ride with my knees, jump up the dust
and iron out the kinks in a green cull's back.
I practiced slappin leather in the barn till I could
hit a pheasant's eye from way 'cross a field.

I'd see them ring-tailed roarers at the bar
like steers makin merry-go-round
in high water, mud in their eyes and like
to die for nothin, and I'd laugh because with a quick
change of duds and saddle I could
bring them to drool like pigs in a peach orchard.
Just because I knew my power as a woman, Pearl.

Now you, you never had to prove yourself enough.
I didn't want you to have to go the same route I did,
in order to be wanted, the way I wanted wanted men,
but I didn't want you to go all soft and stupid.
The world is never going to give you what you need.
Is it too late to tell you that? I take up my pen
now, if it isn't, to tell you, and that goes for love.

When you were learnin to walk, Rosie, I used to laugh
to see you totter and reach for pants legs under
the poker tables. That's over. Now I am sayin enough
is enough. Hang on. Climb up if you can. Plunder.

But don't be lettin them hook their bootheels on your bed.
That's low, Pearl, that's lower than I've ever been.

Come home to me, Pearl. I'd rather you be dead
than on Front Street. Don't go tellin me it's what I've done.

remindin her how I met up with Cole

Texas was full of badmen full of brag and fight
pirootin around them bluffs and yucca. One night a man
called Jesse James came hallooin up to our dugout
hearin we was from Missouri, and with him, hale
as hard money, the brothers Younger, plus Jim Reed.

But my Ma, who never gave me a thing but her bent for headaches
said she wouldn't do for punks, so that left me
to cook up a mess of dough-gob and sop and break
out a can of love apples and flutter my eye,
especially at Cole Younger, him smooth as rattlesnake
root with its milky ooze and his tall moonrise smile,
so blond and so slow . . . I simply took to him
like honeysuckle to fencin, like it does to bloom.

So it's not that I don't remember, Pearl,
what a sudden case of spoons is like, it's that
it just doesn't last, that's all.
And it wasn't all sparkin in the moonlight
loungin with your daddy-to-be whisperin in my ear
I was pretty as a heart flush him lyin there
handsome as an ace-full on kings but
that is how it started out.
Deep down I knew he had about as much use
for me as a hog for a ruffled shirt.
Then he didn't like the looks of me knocked up —
sound familiar? — and then in Liberty, Missouri,
and thereby hangs a tricky tale,
him and Jesse invented bank robbery
American style.
                    In '66 it was and smack on Valentine's Day.

remembering how she turned belly-up

So what if the bluebirds were back and the new
crops of rabbits snufflin under the fuzzy hawbushes
and the bees fiddlin and pokin in the wild plum . . .
that sure ain't no excuse, Pearl!

You were brought up for pure clover, my Pearl,
not for castin yourself at swine and a life
of tough pickins and needles and messes of sprouts.
That's why I packed you off to Chickalah.

So then the crows were fattenin and the umpteenth
crop of rabbits snufflin . . . very next thing I know —
hearin it from a neighbor first — you're all peakish
and undeniably caught with the goods.

I couldn't stomach no blasted event that's why
I went lickety-zip out and found you a livery-man
who'd pay the vet to clean you out and still be willin
to marry. Then you had to go jump the gun
and ankle off to Arkansas to have your bastard leavin me
feelin just like I did when you died behind the lights
in Dallas in the middle of your song — empty empty handed
with the dowry I might have . . . might have . . .

So now you've got your booby prize, Cole's daughter,
and what have I got? I swear I never yet blotted out
a member, but if I find the galoot did this I will
make him worm food at a hand gallop
scatter him like a dose of the wind.

our first Dallas spree continued and ended

We had pretty near all we needed didn't we, Rosie?
I was keepin you safe and supplyin our livery stable
and fancy doins. Everybody knew I had my Pearl.

No one touched you knowin how I was trigger-happy
'til Pa got wind of some fiddlefaddle condemnin me
and stole you right out of your crib in Planter's Hotel
while I was busy down below and with nothin carnal.
So I lit right out for Scyene to get back my baby.

That's when Pa locked me in my room just like he could up
and save me for a proper motherhood and meanwhile
you were grisslin away and Ma was whinin somethin awful
and I was thinkin how I told Jim I smelled a trap
and hopin he might figure out some gallant way to come
get us out of the mess. It was pandemonium.

Ha! I'd got hold of a bread knife halfway fixin on carvin
up my wrists and let the ruby trickle out where they'd see
when I hear that ping on the window and damn me
if Jim Reed isn't climbin up quiet as a rat in a grain bin

with a brandin iron to pry me out and he is grinnin
like a stuffed possum. So I start stompin like a mockey
to hide the racket of crackin wood and before you can say
Goodbye Old Paint I'm Leavin Cheyenne

I'm slidin down the sods and skurtlin through the panic grass
and leavin you, Pearl, with what I can't still choose.

not advisin that this is the proper way

Turns out the whole Fischer gang is out there
in the dark darker'n the inside of a wolf's gut
with even the horses on tiptoes and about to let out
the biggest laugh this side of the Cimmaron.
And I almost have a second thought about my life as I fall
astride a saddle and we all take off like the clatter
wheels of hell shootin in the air, the foxed judge rampagin
on his back porch and with his rusty hog leg jammed,
my gang-in-waitin goin crazy as popcorn on a hot stove,
and then Jim Reed announces we would have the weddin.

So Fischer gets out his Bible II, the outlaw's who's who,
black as a witchcat's overcoat, and solemnly slur-preaches
what to-do marriage is and they wait for me to say I do,

and I do with my mare's flanks heavin as Jim reaches
for my reins and hollers "Ditto!" And so it was done.
That night I married the lot, not one, to be left alone.

remindin her again of the consequences

After that weddin on horseback and all the palaver
about it it didn't take much for Texas to be closin in
on the identity of Jim Reed who when it came to rustlin
had about as much brains as a tin pan has fur.

Then he'd creep home dauncy and sometimes with some pal
on the scout with him, dead bored and chompin their bits
to pieces, like me. One time he brought home this
Cherokee called Sam Starr, six foot five inches tall

who was smilin like a jackass in a haystack.
I dropped my needle.
He was fresh as a breeze of the Territory, Pearl,
with a whiff of blood-revenges, a whiff of maniac.

remindin her how I did come back to her

It wasn't much fun bein stuck out in California
with word out the James gang was there and the banks
sittin with their knees together like virgins.
I was saltier than Lot's wife and Jim was jumpy
as a frog in a skillet and even baby Eddie seemed like
he was on the prod and hankerin for a Texas type
no-questions-asked rendezvous.
                              So back we trekked
about a million miles of drag dust and bad graze
tumbleweed and all-thorn till even my milk was gyppy
figuring how we'd drop by Scyene and get set up
at Pa's brand-artist hideout by pleadin for the baby
and gettin you back, Pearl.

                    I was plenty afraid
you'd have forgot me, Rosie, so it was like a pardon
to a lifer when you ran out to swing from my stirrup
pricklin at least my Ma's heart.
                            Even though the judge
was still techy as a peeled snake seein Jim Reed
and threatenin to comb Jim's hair with his six-gun,
with Jim offerin the judge a halo gratis . . .
                                    But I guess they struck
some sort of Ozark bargain while I was off gatherin
my brains and charms together.
Then Jim went hootin off all happy for Gadshill and I
got left behind as usual.
                    But I had you, Baby.

then what when after that

Jim got a bag on his head and went off with that man —
Wilder or Dickens or Morris — who's supposed to be on the scout
with him — we used to change names easy as a kitten
jumps over a caterpillar —
                            and when that Judas-priest shoots him
they call me as the widow to identify the body

that happens to be left in the sun to cook in its own slime.
Well, I ain't about to let a kiss-cheek collect the bounty.

I am not a woman who cries.
I say I am sorry, Gentlemen.
This is not the body of Jim Reed.
I say you are mistaken.

I left the mistake to be nicely buried.
Jim Reed was one of the littler guys.

here I just want her to know

Dear Pearl, how I wanted you.
I didn't send you off like I sent your brother. I wanted
you to hanker after more . . .
Hell, Pearl, that's sentiment. I flaunted
you on your peacherino
pony and swelled myself up like a carbuncle
to have you sing and dance so
the Dallas stage would clamor: She belongs to Belle.

How was I to know your poor brain would burst
under the limelight? That night was the worst.

seein this heap of writin on my table

I fixed on givin you the straight tips, my Rosie,
all this paper I stained for you — and now it's all
comin back to me unopened . . . I can't figure why
I allowed they'd catch up with you . . . you with Cole
Younger's blood in you and with Jim Reed's folks
providin shelter and then them was all you heard Sam tell
about the lines and lyin low. I say, Dear Pearl,
might as well say Dear Me — Your bastard girl
forces you, rapes from inside . . . No pigsticker
pokes deeper to split the carcass. Child,
with you sendin me back to me still sealed . . .

remindin her how Younger's Bend is her place

I guess you'll forgive me, Pearl, if I try to scribble out
some rhymes. They ain't Byron like I used to read you
but it takes my mind off . . .

Remember how I fetched you and Eddie, darlin, after Cole
leaked out of the landscape into Stillwater? Remember
comin up the windin trail from the river through scrub oak
and locust and hawbushes so thick a bird could hardly turn
itself around to build? You feared Sam Starr at first
with his plucked eyelashes and his high lonesomes,
his wily, crooked smiles. But it was for you, Baby,
I married this land. It was to hide you, my treasure,
under Hi-Early mountain and see you grow with the wild grape
and roses and make dolls from the walnut and red velvet
sumac, cuddle you deep between boulders, persimmon and sycamore.
And it was for you I named it. Younger's Bend.

Remember how you learned to entertain on that old piano
got with the boot from Ogawalla — first job Sam and I
pulled off together — and you didn't mind the jolly company
did you, Baby? All those cow nurses swallow-forkin around
in their low-neck shirts and some old moochers in shoddy
duds but full of ditties and do-funnies to make you laugh
Don't you miss the circus, the giggle-talk and augurin,
badmen gettin flutter-lipped as coyotes? Clappin for my Canadian Lily
just as proud as if it was in some Eastern city. Remember
the even'n "Mr. Wilson from Texas" come crawlin up through
the meadow and I whispered to you "your old friend Jesse James."
You brought him fixins back in our cave all spruced in your rose-
sprigged muslin, remember? I'm just asking you to remember all that,
Rosie, those days of nothin but collectin birds with our eyes,
your yellow hammer, my brown wren, your cardinal, my Bob White,
and on and on, and Eddie out huntin that panther he never found.
I tried to make a home, Pearl.

And it's still here, and I'm still here, and Eddie is like
to tear the place apart without his sister. I'm only askin
that you just trade in your bastard baby for another
chance to be somebody free and unattached with your mother.

Sam Starr and my fiddler

I'd like to know just who Sam Starr thought he was
to pull a face long as a dried snake if ever
I took amusement on my own.

It was Sam who asked that fiddler to our cave stomp
the first time round. 'Course I'd met him in another
life, so it came natural.

The fiddler's not the only one. John Middleton
was a man to ride the river with and I suspect
that Sam doused John that day.

Sam just chuckled when I told him how I found
the body by the Poteau, how buzzards ate
the dead man's eyes and nose.

Then Sam had to go and get himself billed
by Choctaw police as well as Parker's court.
So I did him a special favor

escortin him down to Fort Smith and sweet-talkin Parker.
But Sam had to celebrate his luck
drunk as a Mexican opal

at the Christmas stomp at Aunt Lucy's.
So Sam pulls out his six-shooter and runs it
straight at his cousin Frank.

So Frank doesn't really have a choice.
Sooner'n Satan could light a match both drop.
The fiddler doesn't stop.

He's crackin and I'm feelin ginger in my feet
as I'm liftin up Sam from the foot of that saplin
where he's tryin to hold up death.

Then I leave him and I dance. What else can I do?
But I keep my pearl-handled babies
slappin outside my dancin skirt.

I ain't goin to get more wild than this
and my fiddler knows — so he keeps right on
strokin gut 'til it hurts.

a postscript just in case she reads this in time

Now this ain't remorse, Pearl, but it seems
like my life is a one-story shanty
with a two-story front to it — know what I mean?
I sure wish you were with me.

I'm about as messed up as a red hen
in a pile of cow manure
with everyday wranglin just to prove I've been
despite the jiggered nags and fragglin squalor

alive I guess. Now the only
mount I got that ain't crowbait is this fuzztail
highbinder of a nightmare where a load of turkey
shot blasts me full

in the face and I want to lift my head
and tell you just to tell you . . .
but it is glued down to the mud.
So I reckon your old Ma is just about through

with bein outside of the law.
In the dream, though, I at least have my boots on.
But who, Pearl, if not you,
is goin to wash this body with turpentine and cinnamon

when the time comes? When I am dead,
Pearl, don't let the Cherokee mourners fill
my last hideout with crumbs of stale cornbread.
You know I don't believe I'll

need any such thing to cross
the last river. Just put that fine pistol
Cole gave to me on my heart and cross
my hands over it. As for a will,

Pearl, Younger's Bend has always been
mine, and you must claim your own.

*B*ETSY ROSS

I.

> *— establishing with Powers so disposed — in order to give to*
> *trade a stable course . . . conventional rules of intercourse; . . .*
> *but temporary, and liable to be from time to time abandoned or*
> *varied, as experience and circumstances shall dictate . . .* *

Some say I made it up. Some say not so.
So what? I know that I relive the day —
late May — and may forever — when I met you
with Uncle Ross and Rich Rob. Secretly,

you'd brought me a little piecework to be done
for love and money. I put the kettle on
(for hardly any tea) and we sat down
hush hush — and you brought out the general plan

for a banner, this smudgy doodle you'd made —
not bad. At first I didn't like the a-
symmetry of it. "Too many seams," I said,
"and who wants six-point stars?" I showed how they
could be cut to five: one fold, one snip. I won.
You got your way about the stripes.
                              Tomorrow, then.

---

* All of the epigraphs in this poem come either from George Washington's
notes for his Farewell Address, sent to Thomas Jefferson in May 1792, or from
the Farewell Address itself, delivered in September 1796.

II.

*Taking care always to keep ourselves, by suitable establishments,
on a respectable defensive posture, we may safely trust to tempo-
rary alliances for extraordinary emergencies.*

You came and went and left me with your plan.
    It was heavenly.
All my tricks were ready for your trade:
    seed-stem-crewel-cross-chain
stitch — for you, for me, all signified . . .
    Cut and come again:

You came, to pick it up where you left off.
    You were down to earth
about the price: it's — give or take some — life,
    and all that one was worth . . .

And what a thing to fly
    with you — our seams
far spread-eagle fused —
    our scissions eclipsed.

III.

*'Tis our true policy to steer clear of permanent alliances. . . . let
those engagements be observed in their genuine sense. — But in
my opinion, it is unnecessary and would be unwise to extend
them.*

To begin with, independence is a matter
of one's connections:
               Uncle Ross, for instance,
noticed your lapsing lapel and fray of flounce,
brought my needle to your need, and your

charge to mine. You married money.
Let connections be . . .
               but ours — you broke it.

I did not offer trade to outer-minglers
and keep no secret correspondences.
I have a genuine sense
of past affairs — what makes the present tense

and I'll extend myself — what you forswear . . .

IV.

*. . . so long as we profess to be Neutral, let our public conduct
whatever our private affections may be, accord therewith. . . .*

I never said a word — or spread about
anything more private than our trade
and how in the line of it I made
your specified flag.
             How I feel about

it is something else; of the secrecy that for-
mality is the banner of, one says
nothing, but understands: one simply lays
aside one's foibles —
            passion without form

that might explode the world. A white
swelling under the blue apron is tough
to lay aside however . . .

V.

> . . . In offering to you, my Countrymen, these counsels of an old
> and affectionate friend, I dare not hope they will make the
> strong and lasting impression I could wish — that they will con-
> trol the usual current of the passions . . .

A so-so seamstress and a so-and-so
general do not make up a lasting piece
without some specific drawbacks.
                And now,
and even then,
            our independencies
established, many once-and-for-all-true
accounts lie strangely and — less so — hearsays . . .

and passions —
        yes the passions —
                yes, they too . . .

Having wrung all the loose change out of
the laundry, having put my bottom rags
on the firing lines, having candied the last
cherries and baled all the hay sweet hay
a person could . . .

        I'm ready to snug down
where all the stories start . . .
                    Tomorrow, then.

RINGLING BROS. PRESENT: THE LUCKY LUCIE LAMORT

for China Marks

Between this dream junk wasteland and the Milky Way, I taunt
balance, flaunt it, Lucky Lucie Lamort, Lightbody's
daughter, tiniest funambulist, star of the rag front,
topmost spangles, yeah.

Aren't you stunned by the fine panache
of a life so perfect, so glittery, so up in the air?
Steady as she goes, I love to harp on the hanging threads
of dear faint hearts, my eye on the faithful end
of my own rope, their eyes delivering the quicksilver
energy of their qualms. I boggle, abash, obsess, appall.
I totter to tease . . .
Then, all those indrawn breaths below, the suck of awe
before the fall — not quite — the vibrant adrenalines
in tune, and finally the riot panic of applause,
my extreme unction, yeah.

How I do love the tension of all stretched things:
filaments and wings, the strands and riggings
of the body, the brash fiber of a plucked string.
I dance on pure nerve, live by the corners of my eyes,
by the percipience of my footsole. I am a dazzle machine;
each sequin on me deflects the arrows the stars flick down.
I too am a heavenly body, yeah.

Does my calm repel? Defy? I outgame God and Gravity,
those old hags knitting galaxies. I sit in their spacious laps,
a nonesuch, my moxie a law to myself one hundred feet above
contradiction, that dumb mud that undoes me.
It's neck or nothing, yeah.

How I do love the straightest and narrowest:
I stroll, I spin and trot, I somersault;
I pirouette like Napoleon's pet between the towers
of Notre Dame, where angels fear and gargoyles gape.
I span the volcano's crater in my heatproof suit;
highfalutin as Blondin, I do the useless with élan,
a dare-angel married to Damocles' sword whose stainless
blade I lick clean, yeah.

There was a time I loved the scuff of sawdust and paper trash.
I knew sidewalks, paths through forests, rooms and trains.
Then it happened: I could no longer touch the wide ways
of the world; beneath my knowing feet I felt the mantle
slide, too much to know, and so reboundless, such a drowse
of thumpings, criss-crossed with a disarray
of footings, so untidy; its touch a fatal threat
to the wiring of my gut, yeah.

What a relief, to shinny up the guy, step out on bounce.
I find no falter here where nothing mothers me.
There is nothing like this loneliness, beyond all love.
I walk my rope-long sentences to the turning points.
At every turn my body tangles with eternity;
at every step, anew I learn my center, feel my life
a pattern in the currrent and living web of all.
It is a marriage of letting go and holding on,
a balance of concentration and release, a deepest music
undulating from my toe. It is mathematical, death's friend,
immense, immense . . .

What a weight is the universe. What a caucus
of butterflies and whales, of nebulas and holes.
I put my slipper on its nerve and it answers me
in centimeters, spring and fall, in glitters
at the corners of my eyes, in certain longing
to leave my senses altogether, depart the wire and even air,
rise endlessly and swift to walk the summit
of the solar wind, tramp the rigging
between worlds . . .

I walk the starlight between galaxies,
ride those spinning tops with my heel; I glide
light years to God's labyrinthine ear
like a pure and dizzy prayer.
Yeah.

THE BALLAD OF BASEBALL ANNIE

for Ron Powers

Don't ask me why a passion starts
        Or how, just let me say
One clobbered me two years ago,
        When I first saw Swat play.

The way he swaggered to the box
        And waggled in his stance . . .
The way he stroked the sweet horsehide . . .
        He made the diamond dance.

My room, my heart's all cluttered up —
        Clips, scraps, diary.
I study my gospel scorecards, pray
        And litter, order, sigh.

I hang around the stadium,
        I hang around the bars.
It's full-blown now — but can he see? —
        I am all eyes, all ears.

Annie Burns is the name I give,
        It is my baseball name,
And this diamond life is a life apart,
        and everything but tame.

It's not like where you type all day
        And never score a point.
Its home is not all up in the air.
        Either you're safe or you ain't.

125

My story . . . I go over it
   Again and again, as if
I could make madness plain to you,
   Just plain garden stuff.

The fated field, the devil's pitch,
   The globe, its spin, the sun . . .
It's here we get a glimpse of gods.
   I'm not the only one

I know, but of all us cockeyed gals
   Glued to the diamond tilt,
I am the only one I know
   Who feels this thunderbolt

When Swat whams an apple over the fence,
   Fused with each move he makes:
He shifts a foot, my belly writhes,
   All twisted up with snakes.

A diamond is a girl's best friend.
   Ha Ha — I told you so.
We were engaged at Wrigley Field.
   You are the last to know

How I was the pull behind your whack,
   My hand the one inside
Your mitt, my keen eyes on your balls . . .
   Good luck, my love, God-speed.

Some whiz kid, you, to ditch the Cubs
   And me, your secret Annie.
My room, my heart's still cluttered up
   With you. Why don't you die?

In the loony bin I ponder you
    All twisted up with snakes,
Shot down — is that face mine or yours?
    I guess I've got what it takes.

I make the meaning of my life
    That night at the Edgewater Beach:
I send that note; you answer it.
    At the door, I'm about to reach

For my paring knife, but you slip past.
    I reach my gun. You say
I'm a silly honey to think of this,
    You're such a decent guy.

Point-blank. It's done, and I kneel down
    And hold your hand, your eyes.
I mess my hem in the spill of blood,
    Safe on your sacrifice.

It's here you get this glimpse of gods.
    Here come the flashbulbs, fuzz.
Annie Burns is the name I give,
    Nineteen. And why is because.

I'm finally in on your headlines, Swat,
    Closer than any wife.
That's just why I got that hotel room,
    That's why I brought the knife.

The bullet was for me, I swear.
    According to my plan:
First I'd cut you up, then blast
    Myself — we'd die as one.

I missed your heart by just an inch —
    How lucky — just enough
To make a miracle, beyond
    Just plain garden stuff.

I wasn't safe 'til you filled me up
    Like God fills up a saint.
The game's much like. You're in or out.
    Either you're safe or you ain't.

My diamond life may be fouled away,
    But my split-skinned heart's still fair.
Who doesn't know that Annie Burns,
    When this cursed play is over,

Will rise right up from Kankakee
    And start all over again,
With hits and catch-as-catch-can and breaks
    For home, as some light-fingered man?

I'd do anything to flaunt us back,
    To all your fans out there
Who love to watch me, win or lose.
    My heart's still tingling bare,

Scraped garish as it was in court,
    bright gush daubed on newsprint, too.
America in its nutshell — Love,
    Warheads, Hullabaloo;

Split-second affairs, your bang-bang plays,
    The spin you lock on the globe,
Your violence-laced tenderness,
    All this jazz and sob . . .

My story . . . I go over it
    Again and again like a game
I put on *your* glamour with my crime.
    But I won't accept no shame.

For she's a jolly good fellow
    Who can say to passion: DIE.
A diamond is a girl's best friend
    That nobody can deny.

*T*HE HOTTENTOTTE VENUS

Above the brains whose salient folds were thought,
post mortem, worth pickling for future study, squat three
less quizzed Victorian glass bell jars; here float
the only female specimens the wizard Cuvier

thought worth sequestering in Formalin, as human
proof how bodies gauge and render regnant graces.
He labelled our variants thus: *la peruvienne*,
la negresse, and strangest of all, *la Venus
Hottentotte*. Doctor Cuvier himself cut straight
to the heart the matter with *la Venus*, probed muscle
for that bone our Big Brains supposed braced her rarest trait,
hid deep in the marvelous mounds of flesh that bustled

behind every shift of her body, from posing nude
to rattling her freak-cell bars. Up from boneless muscle,

his scalpel prized this rare pliant piece of booty instead.

DEAR LYDIA E. PINKHAM

for Robert Pack

I am always dying and it makes no difference.
— E. B. Browning

10 West Fourteenth Street
New York City
1 April, 1897

Mrs. Lydia E. Pinkham
Lydia E. Pinkham Medicine Co.
Lynn, Massachusetts

Dear Mrs. Pinkham: I hesitate to take
my pen in hand, or waste your time with this,
but I'd like a woman's ear, one hundreds have
confided in, if one can trust the papers.
I do not find the ads for Lydia E.
Pinkham's Vegetable Compound "obscene
and titillating" (as my husband does).
My maid seems healthy, and the cook tells me
she's been drinking Pinkham's every day
for the last month. (The cook won't touch it though,
because of the alcohol.) My husband's friend,
Dr. Thorstein Fallis, famous young
gynecologist, has treated me
for years. He blames my "naughty ovaries"
for all: the fits and faints, the weeping laughter . . .

Ever since my honeymoon (five years)
I've suffered cravings, backache, nausea,
suppression of the "turns" — would you agree
it's from the ovaries? Those sweet pink hearts?

And that's not all. He says my womb's inspired
inconsequent behavior, petulance,
caprice and lying artfulness, plus tense
lassitude. And last, not least — I'm told —
"the solitary vice." I have been warned,
insanity is but a step from this.

It may be crazy to sing to your ovaries,
still, I do, as I don't have a child.
In the dark, my dark, I see pale fists
of unborn faces, turned up toward my heart,
plump fruits, my wanderlusts. Till now I fear
I have been too content to be no more
than an invalid, achieving neither cure
nor death. I move in neurasthenic circles
descanting symptoms with even sicklier women
(thus being indisposed does pass the time).
I've tried warm baths and cold baths, abstinence
from spicy food. I've tried electrical,
mesmeric, hydropathic, chemical
fads and fashions, from plugs to pessaries.

But what I really want to ask I fear
is something I can't mention to my friends.
It's when my doctor starts his "medical
manipulations" testing for those known
unnatural responses that imply
derangement of the female organs. When
he strokes here, then there, inserting his
newfangled slowly sliding speculum,
I jerk and weep. "Aha!" says he. "Don't be
afraid. I am an expert with the knife.
The operation is quite simple, Dear."
It's called "female castration," and if I don't
improve by fall, he says, we'll have to try it.
Is this what you call "belly-ripping" or
is Dr. Fallis right, that it will help

clear and elevate my moral sense,
save me from gluttony and just cussedness?
(I feel a pressure on the little cup
of my collarbone and my heart begins to beat
in every organ, every fingertip,
when Thorstein Fallis treads my stair and knocks.
The walls tilt in, and objects in my room begin
to leer — ebony looms and ormolu
clock, woolwork portraits, gas jets, polished grates —
accuse, accuse, creep closer, sneer like nurses.)

I itch. And yet I fear the knife, the "death
of Woman in the woman," death in life.
I quiver and toss; my womb is all a-prance,
Is there any feeling in a female frame
that cannot be or signify an illness?

It is not ladylike to be in love.
I hope I'm not, but when that doctor comes,
whose hands have been beneath my petticoats,
I must tear my hair, contort my limbs and howl . . .

Once I bit dear Thorstein's hand. It bled.
But he's bled me! When the curse it pleased the Lord
to grant to Woman ceased in me that man
stuck his leeches to those . . . lips; they sucked
down there until I swooned. It didn't help.

I try to be a perfect blend of puppy
and princess, frail, yet built for childbirth, dumb,
just hopelessly flawed, meant "ceaselessly to suffer
from love's eternal wound" as I make tea
and knit. Hired for the price of a ring: I do
nothing, and I do it splendidly . . .

Malingering is "one expensive hobby,"
Charles would have it, who used to love my pallor —
spiritual, so beautiful, but now
wants a son, he wants a wife who meets
her "marital appointment" more than seldom.
I've seen his eyes go straying toward my maid.
(Why are the females of the lower classes
so healthy?) Take Dorcas now: she's just eighteen
of course, the type they call a "buxom lass,"
straight from the country, milk-fed, brash.
At first I didn't think she had a nerve
in her body, but the New York pace
may have infected even her. (Else why
is she using Pinkham's every day?)
I've wondered if she might not be in love —
the vulgar blushes, the silly songs she hums
or whistles thoughtlessly all day. I think
robust vitality is crude somehow.

I wouldn't want to die in perfect health,
but how long can I balance on this edge?
As if I didn't have enough to see to,
Dorcas sometimes sulks — but only till
Charles comes home. Oh, then she is on top
of the world and saying how very good I look,
don't I? At times I am perturbed by this:
I dream she's coupling in my bed, and with
my husband. Winking from the dark skylight,
I feel my fingers chill and chill creeps up
my arms and when it hits my heart I start
to laugh, and then I sink away. It seems
my arousal is my fall. Forgive me, dear
Mrs. Pinkham, for running on. It does
relieve my mind to write, but just so long
as Dr. Fallis don't find out. The world
is nervous and my skin is thin. Do tell

me if the Pinkham brew will fix me up.
"A Baby in Every Bottle" is what you say.
Could you be clear just how this works?
With what I've told you, can you recommend
a course of treatment, or is my case past hope?
Looking to your answer, I remain
Your supplicant, Triphena Twitchell-Rush.

                              10 West 14th St.
                              Apr. 1, 1897

Dear Lydia E. Pinkham, I haven't got
no friends to turn to. I just come to town
not but four months since. My father passed
away from his heart, my mother from her womb.
We was always poor. Now I have trouble
with both my heart and womb. The place I got
is with this fancy doctor's family, but
seeing as how his wife is always sickly
and doctors coming here like fruitflies round
a rotten peach, I don't think it does
no good to ask a doctor. She ain't better.
(Sometimes with all their help I figure she's worse.)
I hope I haven't caught what ails the Mrs.
from the windows always being closed in there
and listening all day long to this and that
complaint. And then I overhear the doctor
say that reading novels is a cause
of uterine decay and lesions with
The Castle of Otranto right there by
her sofa, and me reading it to her
a week now. Could that cause "congestion of
the ovaries," like I seen in the letters
to you in the paper? I've got dragging down
and filled up feelings and the returns has stopped

for near on three months now, from almost when
I come to this place. So I want to ask
will your tonic that dissolves and throws out
tumors and brings on the monthly flow
(I think there's something in me sucking all
my strength) restore me? I've been using it
a month or so and so far I'm the same.

And maybe you could give an opinion on
my mistress, she is one of those high-strung
types, real pale, and even sipping tea
seems to fatigue her, but, oh, she's beautiful
as some fairy princess, golden hair and hands
the light goes trembling through, but then she faints.
(She never goes too far from something soft
to fall on.) The other day she flipped and flopped
herself around like a hooked fish and screamed
what I daren't write. And then the doctor said,
"We'll have to shave her head," and so she stopped.
Then he whispered to me and the master, "Fear
is a sedative." I wonder. I toss all night
'til the bed is all of a topsy-turvydom,
and after those nights I can't keep down no food.
It's dreams: in one I saw a "female organ"
blown up like a balloon and rising right
into the sky; and the doctor comes with one
of them pointed poles for picking up stray trash
and stabs it, and gray worms rain down on me.

It's been three months since all of this began.
I'd ask the master, seeing how he is
a doctor, but (I don't know if I should
say this part) I am afraid of him
since almost the first night that I was here
and he came by my room, asking for pity

and I was helpless . . . Well, that is enough.
A poor girl just can't ask that class of man
even if . . . and I don't know, this thing . . .

What I only have to know is does your tonic
clean out the womb, eventually, and soon?
Should I use the Sanitive Wash and Syringe?
Do you think I will "go smiling through"?
I anxiously await your answer. I
remain, Your humble servant, Dorcas Flowers.

                                    10 West 14th Street
                                    New York City
                                    4 July, 1897

Dear Mrs. Pinkham: Here am I again
If I'm not cured, I don't know what I am.
So here's my testimonial. I've heard
that every woman who's dissatisfied
with her lot is sick — well, they just haven't tried
to liquidate that lot with Mrs. Pinkham's
Vegetable Compound. And thank you for
the little book. I used to hate descriptions
of anatomy. (I blushed to mention
even a table's *leg*.) Now I am full
as a Chinese toy shop, caught in my own web
of defects, and I love them. When I've had
my daily dose, I dare my Charles to peek
at "Teeny Pheeny" (Sshhhh — it's my pet name)
and I don't care when he storms out to his club.
I don't mind that Dorcas is blowing up
under her apron, for I know she took
a good deal of your recipe, and I
need only wait and meanwhile lull myself
with nothings tra la la la la la la la. . . .

My brain feels polished, put up on a shelf,
while my womb is fortified with your
magic potion, does my thinking for me.

(Dr. Fallis would say that this is health.)
Idleness is an art; the uterus is
a sewer, tra la. I dreamt I heard a door
forced below so I went down to . . . He
Himself, as big as death. (I recognized
his cufflinks, though he wore a mask.) He bore
a satchel, stuffing it with all I would
not sacrifice. ("You're ill to the degree
you own yourself!") I see a trail of blood,
its source between his legs. He said, "It's not
my body but my heart," so I say, "Good,
we'll cut it out." And then he died, tra la.

Sometimes I think that Charles has married Dorcas.
Sometimes I think perhaps she has my child
in her oven, or I'm their child. When Charles comes home,
he always wants to know why why why . . .
he finds me singing softly in the closet
behind the row of boots (Well, that is where
I keep you, Mrs. Pinkham, darling, cases).

The dark gets full of swirling colors; they
take shape in a fine ballet of oozing cells;
I tell myself these are the true untried
ovarian forms of thought, the nerves in air
ramified by my relationship
to my "mother's milk." I haven't given up
my life of symptomania (where is
the poet of pathology? oh, yes:
Mrs. Browning, healthy compared to me)
nor animal economy, the commotions of
my tender tubings, oval agents, woe

manifold, nor infinite Fallopian . . .
O my. O you, in your black silk and white
fichu, they say you are a table-rapper
and a quack, those doctors! pooh! with their heroic
gulping purges, blisters, laudable pus . . .

I am a riddle, Terra Incognita,
as far as Charles is concerned, queen of the clumsy
tangle, a house within a house, an engine
within an engine. La! It takes just three
bottles a day to keep me going. I
used to be afraid of the chloral faces
in window curtains, I'd whimper down the dark
keyhole, cave . . . Now each day "Pinkham's lark"
(that's what I call the winglike sweep
across my brain when I'm behind the boots)
brings me to my mission, to be happy
with my lot. I sit and concentrate
on moon and tides. My mind's a Pandora's box.
Hope's the only evil left in it.

It's Independence Day, and Dorcas cares
for me. Let's all be free with love and all
things out of our control. I'll take as much
of the doctor's nostrum as Dorcas measures out.
More than one life is in the willing hands
I will to her. Mrs. Pinkham, I am
so happily sorry for the length of this.
I might have been a writer, but a woman
must write with blood, and I'm too weak to spare
blood, even with your tonic in my veins.
But I'm mostly cured. I don't care what I'm not.
With blessings on you, Mrs. Pinkham, I
remain myself, Triphena Twitchell-Rush.

SIMONE WEIL: HUNGER'S FOOL

I. *Dialogue (Paris, 1914–23)*

> *Follow my resigning;*
> *That as I did freely part. . . .*
>
> *Ah! no more: thou break'st my heart.*
> — George Herbert, "A Dialogue"*

Love's necessity — food for a child.
    I wanted to be hungry like a man
    fighting for the truth.
                At five I mailed

my sugar to the front.
              Is it human —
refusing sweetness? Fusing it with pain?

A body's obligation — to obey
    gravity: O let me be walked over
    like the earth, the enemy . . .
                How could we
treat men like dirt?
            I wash with cold water
to test my trembling; at play I'd rather falter

than slap my brother. He slaps me. It's agreed.
Real headaches strike and blind with woman's blood.

Desire, not brains, lures truth. Love's pain: ersatz
sanctity. Love's body: broken klutz.

---

* All epigraphs to the poems are from George Herbert's long poem *The Temple: Sacred Poems and Private Ejaculations.* George Herbert (1593–1633) was Simone Weil's favorite poet, and these were her favorite poems.

II. *Providence (Paris, 1924–29)*

The trees say, Pull me: but the hand you stretch,
Is mine to write, as it is yours to raise.

— "Providence"

They say I was a pretty child, but now . . .
I have the power to change. A mind or two,
pockets spilling tobacco, myopia,
studied misfitting — I don't have to go

outside myself to find out what is foreign
to me. It's time. No dancing — never learned.
Walking with friends — the plums — their red perfection . . .
They dared me to climb the wall, to shake some down.

I did, but getting down myself was harder.
One stretched out his arms to me — I turned
plum protean — shook my head — damned the hunger
that got me into this. I shook all over.

Crawled down alone.
            Why do I feel that touch
of shame? Why . . . ?
            "Twelve o'clock: it's time for lunch."

III. *Bitter-Sweet (Roanne and St. Etienne, 1931–34; Paris, 1934)*

> *I will complain, yet praise:*
> *I will bewail, approve:*
> *And all my sowre-sweet dayes*
> *I will lament, and love.*
>
> — "Bitter-Sweet"

They didn't like my sniffy monotone
staccato, putting a foreign accent on
my mother tongue; they didn't like that, done
with school, I went out as the Red Virgin.

Still, I managed to teach their children,
who loved me.

        Can you solder a joint? No?
Well, there's a gap in your education,
mes semblables.
        "You're fired," they said. And so?

In every mode of life there is a rhythm
to be loved.

        Work that's botched is less
boring. The electric works in Paris
taught me other things. When my furnace
scorched my arms, the welder smiled. Grace is
knowing, sharing slavery, is genius.

IV. Justice (Paris and Portugal, 1935)

> Why should I justice now decline?
> Against me there is none, but for me much.
>
>   — "Justice"

No more than mascot for the toughs, clumsy
confrère, fragile eccentric, talking a red
streak around blue moons as far as they
are concerned . . . with me, I don't mean to confuse

them. They know that. It's myselves I confuse.

Then there is that divine Wednesday — out of
a job myself — meeting those two fitters,
one young, one old—chatting hobbies above
our hunger, passions above our pain. Reading,

I said, is mine. (They smile.) All life is reading.

Later, on a middle-class holiday
in Portugal — alone — full moon — poor fishing
village — women with candles (a saint's day
procession) chanting. Now I see: a slave

is a natural Christian. I, a slave.

V. Denial (Spain, 1936)

> Each took his way; some would to Pleasures go,
> Some to the warres and thunder
>   Of alarms
>
>   — "Denial"

Klutz as I am, I will not be left out
of Spain's mad fumbles. As an Anarchist
I see that any group can make a Beast
of a persuasion: "A village voted that

the earth was round." Tyrants! Flat truths are still
cooked up alone, as I proved that August:
left behind in woe-man's land, crossed, washed
in the blood of Aragon, saved by the spill

of boiling oil from boiling blood . . . Why please
the dead? They swallow everything — cold
chasms — revolution is the people's
opium.
           And all that parts, it's true,
links also.
           This intelligence? — is strangled
in fatigues.
           I limp home — failed cook — it's true.

VI. *Faith (Italy, 1937)*

> *Hungrie I was, and had no meat:*
> *I did conceive a most delicious feast;*
> *I had it straight, and did as truly eat,*
> *As ever did a welcome guest.*
>   — "Faith"

Beauty is not to eat. I looked for hours
toward the Last Supper. I studied it,
its twofold recipe, one flat, the other
three-dimensional; in both, the point

is central, one who gives himself to eat.
Necessity is space. I thought for days
about Michelangelo's *Night* and *Dawn*,
those slaves. Muscles of our geometries.
Works and measures. Between any one

and another a space must be left open

for God to flow in. In a café in Milan
the waiter peered at my postcards. He smiled.
Perspectives. I was so happy. Eve began
the mess, bit beauty, swallowed and was soiled.

VII. *Redemption (the heart of the mind, 1938)*

> *At length I heard a ragged noise and mirth*
> *Of thieves and murderers: there I him espied,*
> *Who straight, your suit is granted, said, & died.*
> — "Redemption"

When the thief Love enters, he must also break
a heart.
                    One night he comes and takes me — back
to his place
                    with him, I climb to his attic,
stand before
                    his window where he makes me — look
out past scaffoldings and riverboats —
the world's business.
                    One table, two chairs, loaves
of bread, and wine:
                    we stretch out on bare boards
now and then
                    to rest; between full buds
and winter, cold light and joy, we loll and chat.
He promised
                    to teach me things. But he forgot.
One day,
                    the sun-and-earth taste in my mouth
        still,
                    he said, "Go now," and threw me out.

My heart in shreds, I wandered the streets and knew
I couldn't find that room again. He was through.

VIII. *The Bunch of Grapes (near the Rhône, 1941)*

> *Blessed be God, who prosper'd Noah's vine,*
> > *And made it bring forth grapes good store,*
> > *But much more him I must adore,*
> *Who of the Law's sowre juice sweet wine did make,*
> *Ev'n God himself being pressed for my sake.*
>
> — "The Bunch of Grapes"

The city's occupied. A Jew can't teach
them anything — Christ knows — so here I am,
picking grapes in Saint-Marcel d'Ardèche,
learning the earth. *Amare amabam.*

Babylonian — the Rhine valley,
its shadows, my fatigue. I play I am
a shepherd, say the paternoster day
in and out, in Greek. I eat the rhythm

of the stars, translate my "daily" bread
as "supernatural" crumb. *Amare am-
abam.* A space opens in the vineyard
to surround my prayer as my body's claim

does purple work. Thank Vichy greed. I am
famished, fit. *Amare amabam.*

IX. *Discipline (Marseilles, 1941)*

> *Love is swift of foot;*
> *Love's a man of warre,*
> > *And can shoot,*
> *And can hit from farre.*
> > — "Discipline"

After the fall in   pity's paralysis
beyond the body   and its instruments —
the ship, the blind man's   cane, the sacraments —
waiting for the light,   the light that is

supernatural to the blind,   to change,
I am   at the intersection of
time and space as always.   They say if
I cross over   there may be a chance

from New York to cross   to London, join the op-
position there —   and form the nursing corps
I dream of — the Virgin   milk, the blood and water
sent to the front . . .

           The eternal light does not
change, as the wind   battering ships does not
calm down, or mind. . . .
                  I try to focus, hope.

X. The Collar (New York, 1942)

> I struck the board, and cry'd, No More.
> I will abroad.
> What? Shall I ever sigh and pine?
>
> — "The Collar"

Conquerors are dreamers. I dream too.
I've volunteered for any sort of mission,
as long as it feeds my need; my only weapon
is weakness — and predilection for the true

self-effacement — if only . . . (it is the clue
to creation, you know — the abandon-
ment of God, the secret presence).   One
day they will grant it, also listen to

my nursing plans. Forlorn, I'm crossing over
on the *Valaaren*. Folklore, quantum theory,
Harlem Baptists, the anguish and plenitude
of New York: a void to me. Give me danger.
I'm pagan, but I'd bear salt baptistry.
Still better, give up to darkness *and* for good.

XI. *Affliction (London, 1943)*

> *Now I am here, what Thou wilt do with me*
>> *None of my books will show:*
> *I reade, and sigh, and wish I were a tree;*
>> *For sure then I should grow*
> *To fruit or shade: at least some bird would trust*
> *Her household to me, and I should be just.*
>
> — "Affliction"

London at last. No holiday. For me
a holy day is ten hours spent digging
potatoes; a rapture would be gathering
thistles in my bare arms in Normandy.

And now I would feed my people, bleed in fields
if I had my way. When *will* the Free French trust
my hunger? In Holland Park, my messy nest
annoys the kind landlady. Attention! Birds

keep life in the branches over Princedale Road.
It's lovely, really, but . . .
                                    always the empty
margins where I live goad thought: to see
space is to grasp one's proto-work. Sainthood

ought to be the pattern for a life
available to anyone. A peasant's wife . . .

XII. *Affliction Still (London, 1943)*

> *Once a poore creature, now a wonder,*
> *A wonder tortur'd in the space*
> *Betwixt this world and that of grace. . . .*
>
> *My thoughts are all a case of knives.*
>
> — "Affliction"

Like certain insects, I am the color
of dead leaves. The weight and influence
of injustice seems to decrease with distance
for all but me. Their gravity? And where

is the formula? My own myopia
defies it. In Paris the children have no fruit.
Can I eat apples here? They need — at the front —
plasma, nurses. No distant algebra

ever measured an earthly tragedy
as Greeks by scales, geometry, that "daughter
of labor's fortitude." Antigone.
Proverbs and fools. Should I bury my brother?

What is beautiful is anonymous.
The village idiot is a genius.

XIII. *Love (Middlesex Hospital, 1943)*

> *You must sit down, sayes Love, and taste my meat:*
> *So I did sit and eat.*
> — "Love"

Why must we be cannibals in love?
My soul, I confess, has craved a pomegranate
seed, and even this is carnal. Eve
began it: wanting, loving only what

one can eat; but to love purely is
to love another's hunger. A human gift.
It is too much to hold: pain, genius, mass
and single soul. The nurses chide — can't lift

a spoon — their sad fruit fool — too sweet — give me
Lear's sort — the truth — the nakedness that's close
to death because unveiled where truth must be
hidden. I'm a fool without eating fools, God knows.

A grain of mustard seed is the smallest of
all seeds. My dearest condiment . . . for love.

$\mathcal{M}$ARIA MITCHELL*

I.

Our female eyes are unsurpassed. Earth turns
civil through tiny stitches, seeds, pins, dust
tamed, shadow boxes, kitchen countings . . . Trust
me, this finicky eye toward Heaven discerns
well: nebulae, pearl-edged, and hazy Saturn's
tattings, lace fainter than spiderwebs. I keep
house now with my telescope. I sweep,
from one 'til dawn, the skies. My eye learns
which colors vary, which specks wander far
beyond our own ellipse. I trace the eclipse,
exact and spectral, seek "the interior
planet" behind the shadow tossed to earth.
From sun to sun . . . What good is work if it's
not infinite? I kneel at a creator's hearth.

II.

Did I miss a man and children? Since you are
a woman, and kind enough not to be too shy
to ask a stranger, I will . . . I will try to answer.
I'm tired. This train's so slow. Now. What to say.
I've been so busy, always. Still, the sky
can be a cold companion; a short affair
with a comet can leave one warm, but empty.

---

* Maria Mitchell (1818–89), daughter of an astronomer, received, in 1847, the
gold medal offered by the King of Denmark for the first discovery of a telescop-
ic comet. In 1848, she was the first woman to be elected to the American Acad-
emy of Arts and Sciences.

When you come home alone after the honor,
lionized, fêted, you can, quite suddenly,
want to put your arms around someone,
and there is nothing but the infinite
in your heart — no leap, no embrace. And then, the dawn
wipes out your closest friends. The northern lights
are fickle. The variable stars do not call out
for milk. I wonder . . . You, you tell me about it.

Part Four $\mathcal{V}$ IEWING THE BODY

Ashamed, one asks, should a corpse be viewed
or not?

—Rahel Varnhagen

$\mathcal{A}$ LITTLE PLAY FOR ST. VALENTINE'S DAY

When Zeus discovered that Prometheus, a mortal, had stolen Olympian fire for human use, his revenge took the form of a gift: Pandora. Zeus asked each of the gods to contribute to the manufacture of this most beautiful, malicious, and capricious female. When complete, she would be sent to Prometheus with a closed box, containing all the evils of the world, including delusive hope. Both Prometheus and Pandora knew that her gift box, as part of the deal with Zeus, was never to be opened. An old story.

Preface: Her Riddle

I represent a law, but not the First.
(The First Law works, and I am there for fun.)
The gods made the best of me the worst;
I am Hot Stuff, but farthest from the Sun.

For every single motion: my minimum
is never nil; my maximum is One.
As far as History goes, I am Big Time.
For every sloven rhyme I am the Reason.

I am myself a "unified desire
for parting" as the scientists like to say;
that is, I'm part and parcel, mirror and mire
of passion passing. I get carried away

by the Accident of Order, but I fly
out as Order After. *Who am I?**

---

* Entropy, the Second Law of Thermodynamics.

I. Setting the Scene

Things were cool before Prometheus
got the urge to set the world on fire
and lacking his own spark pilfered one from Zeus
who thought so little of getting even (after

all, why should he mess with a punk, pure sun
being under his thumb?) that, with his genius
for the most brilliant mortifications,
he made me — namely — the offer none can refuse:

a gift bearing gifts, in return for a burglary.
The world was dubious — I seemed too good
to be true, with my vulcanized symmetry,
Olympian charms and (not least) hope chest. Shrewd

Zeus said: "You wanted fire — why settle for less
than the whole shebang?" Such was Zeus' original
                    forgiveness.

II. The Main Character

A word about the box — you know I didn't get it
(like the too-good joke it was), knowing what
was in it for me, but I thought that maybe
something was — ambrosia, my trousseau,
music or jewels — hell — I didn't know.

There's nothing now — just one grouchy scrap of hope
that didn't manage to fly out like the rest
of Plaguesville, being slow and not too bright.
Still, the bleater's lonely —
                    my chest's made for more than one . . .

Between us, I am your curiosity.
In spite of Promethean Progress I can't keep the lid
on its reverse. Perhaps I am your dream,
as all in all and all over you have to admit:

there's something in almost all those getting out.

III. *The Supporting Cast*

But wait — there's something else to be said for me:
I am the *original* package deal — your bonus
onus and boredom's bane. I could be your free
lunch, your Cracker Jack toy, your Vitamins Plus

Irony. My first name's Pandora Mud,
but call me what you like as long as my All-
Giving is implied: Soup Kitchen, Crude
Oil, Little Miss Sunshine, Moonshine, Plurabelle . . .

I follow stolen fire, War & Glory, Progress.
I'm Ultra, Super, Natural; Bag & Baggage.
I am the strut, bed, and truss of your Gross
Universal Product, a hope-crammed outrage.

So whatever you beg-borrow-steal I'll be
along — please, let me oblige you — C.O.D.

IV. *The Final Free Play*

I had even less choice than you, Promo Pet,
sent into the world bearing zip save excuses,
not mine — given; with all I have to give — no treat,
a trick, and punk to boot! I wasn't my own idea.

You move me only through the cruddy chaos
you are yourself moving through me. Between us,
I'd love to be more than your van of intangibles,
more than a flirty piece of unoccupied space,
miniature of Heaven, each feature framed and empty.

Olympus called me their rummage, loose tally
of handy odds and ends not even gods can bear
to throw away, their "Mixtrash Compoodle." Yours Truly
dropped out of this . . . confined disorder . . .
                    and Hell — what a Mother is she.

V. *The Acts to Follow*

So. I'm all abroad now, and every mouth
who gossips me guilty I presume is just as hungry
as ever for my gifts. Want to know what else
I've managed to open up besides the old box?

Just look at your eyes — what a sight! — all agog
and awonder. And I've seen your eyebrows shrug.

Of course I'm all out of sorts when whole worlds are
pleased as pigs to look right through me. As if
I were not the prime sweepstakes and all-time door-
prize, every last blankety-blank filled out, sent off

leaving you to your toy designs . . .
                            What a laugh!

Here's another way to play It: there I am
the nova hung lightly and low on uranium ropes
giving out at their ends but meanwhile the sky's
an open oven, love, and its heats are hopes —

the quick and thievish kind like Prometheus'
in-and-out between-the-lines ever so after
all that the whole show is after all over.

CIRCE

for "Perseus"

Circe and Odysseus confront each other. He has come to her palace to retrieve his shipmates, all of whom Circe, an ace witch, has turned into swine. After a year of pleasure, Odysseus decides it is indeed time to set out again for Ithaca. Circe serves as travel agent.

I.

Because your men were making pigs of themselves,

that's why. And for fun.

                 Notice, there's room in the sty
for at least one more . . . beast?

              Look sharp! —

                    Those wolves —
I made them; the lions too. They've all come to stay,
though they think like men (I could hardly change their minds)
that they can beguile me.

               What oinks and whines!
Have you ever heard a pig try to purr? Well.

                 It lends

a certain pathos to the place — no?

             The sun's
my father. I inherited his lack
of pity, only a degree of his power.   Like him,
I love to captivate, in my way,   turn back
evolution a bit now and then,   at whim.

But you look antsy. You look mad in fact.
Come in.   Let's talk.

              It's only the first act.

II.

Right. That's my loom in the hall. I sing, I weave . . .
uh . . . "curtains."

               Most middle-class witches do
bizarre and gift crafts on the side.

               Don't leave.
Stay. Wallow for a while.

               I just might spare you
the angst of sailing home alone.

               Disarm
yourself, for Pan's sake!

               Tell me about your war,
your lovers, et cetera. Try to match my charm
and I might do you a favor.

               Here, let me pour
a drop of honey wine for you —

               Aeaea's own.
"Aeaea" means "land of wailing." I didn't name
the place. It's also known as "Isle of Dawn."
Surely you will stay 'til sunrise?

               Don't blame
me . . . sleepy, Darling? Here's one final touch
I hate to give.

               So much for that.   So much.

III.

Dingbust! No change?

               Hog Sugar! — who gave you rue?
Priss-petal and raven root — the one anti-potion
I can't outcharm.

               But, entre nous,
I'm kind of glad.

               I've wanted a distraction
from the offhand makeshift metamorphosis
of men.

If you want to know, I've had it up
to here in half-lit half-wit magic trash,
this grunting bothersome stock.
                    My empty cup,
see, runneth over: *abracadabra* — — —
                    gush.
I had no grounds for revenge. Do you?

No stock in men, no men in stock — this was
a problem.
                    Seduce me now, though: unbutton, undo
our loneliness. Look, I'll put this moly-flower
in my hair, mercurial.
                    You'll stay, my dear?

IV.

I made both the palace and zoo with words. I talked
myself into them. It's a gift, but you have to practice,
drill, drill, drill.
                    But there you are, intact
without my say-so.
                    I guess you can do what you please.
So. Here we are.
                    Your crew brought round, my wand
snapped in two. Let's celebrate. Here's wine
(no tricks), a bath, a purple quilt . . . Let's find
and loose us in luxury, like ruse-lovers, twine
and twine to be.
                    Of course I know. I know you will
leave me . . .
          speechless.
                    You'll think you dreamed
me, tell Penelope how you and the boys
came down with a bug, a syndrome with the name
of Circe-lethargia. You were laid up a year.
Will you suffer me this last honest dance, my dear?

V.

I send you by way of Teiresias; you must
know what you are about.

> You've made enough

false starts. Agreed?

> I've taught you a little trust

in dalliance is not a bad thing. But love
and play alone won't get you home.

> So run

along:

> with the North Wind to the Ocean Stream,
> past the stand of willows Persephone (that
> great yawn of girl) likes so much.

> Here, kill a ram

and ewe the color of sun eclipsed (which I
will kindly provide, sweet pig, as an offering
to Hell without you).

> Make sure you wave away

all the blood-curious ghosts — they'll cluster
for sips and thrills.

> *Then, wait for the he that's she*

to down a shot of blood.

> *S/he will tell you about the Sea.*

VI.

As if you didn't know: Your end will come
from this:

> waves swell around Aeaea now,

a million nodding heads and reaching limbs.
What the reaching and nodding are for, you'll know
soon enough. It's not for me to tell.

> To Hell

with you.

And so it goes.

                  Your double-trouble hero's
death goes with you, the stink and sty of mortal
self-pity, among other pastimes.
                          Here, this breeze
is for you. I made it, take it. To nudge you on
toward . . .
                  "Perpetual Dusk" they call it, I call it
"Persephone's Biffy."

                  Do stop on your return.

                • • •

A quick trip, indeed!
                  And off again?
                          Sunk twice,
I won't get over this.
                  Just one more kiss.
Advice: avoid Sirens —
                  tramps compared to me.
So. So long.
                  The willows' sea crows know this much:
even a witch can feel —
                  the finishing touch.

$\mathcal{W}$OMAN WITH GARDENIA

for Barry Schactmann, his "life class"

Breda, as usual, has struck a tricky pose,
typically classic, flexed, her peculiar aplomb
part dance part factious sway, a grace almost
as hard to capture as hold — as hold she must
for thirty minutes. From where I am, I'm damned
if I can see the quandary in her torso's
tilt toward me, one arm crooked out too near
eye level for me to get straight, the other somehow
inclined (away from me) in a trenchant gesture
                    toward the opposite window.

Her head is in the way. Her hair is rimmed
in dazzle, a backlit cloud. And set in this central
blurred tendril drift is just what I want to draw.
For Breda's not all nude — today's gardenia
appeals to the novice in me, against the rule
our class breaks most: a figure rashly trimmed
before its naked imperatives — planes
and volumes, spaces and motion — are in place
maligns the gift of a blank page. Scars, chains,
                    nipples, birthmarks — all banned.

Gardenias, too. I know that much. But still,
the light that gets around her hair slips in
between rust curls and petals of the gardenia
informally poked between her ear and the
skull's templar bone, whose plane and tilt make clear
the head's relation to the sternum's angle,
its rib cage slanting likewise, determining
the shoulders' starting points, the neck's, the spine,
the pelvis' twist, knees, feet . . . and everything
                    a gardenia won't help align.

It's difficult to look and be so clearly
outside the action, removed from the body that counts here
with all its heart — not only the minutes left
to hold, but on making its living — that and a gift
apparent even to the talentless: the pure
and barely stricken sense that there's a story
on hold here, poised in a crucial facet, maybe
telling all. Our time is going fast,
the nose of my conté crayon on our paper body
                    going nowhere, hard-pressed.

Some lines are always, I've learned, by nature more
unstable than others. Of course, your straight up-standing
verticals and horizontals, level,
best moor a figure in its frame — how tall
or far, or close or dear to the one who's drawing
the one who's drawn may be. Unperpendicular
to these, the slants will seem comparatively
exploitative of space, moving to rise,
fall, teeter, even to tears . . . and shove's as likely
                    as push. How calm she is!

Tick tock. Tick tock tick. No one would ever say
our Breda's easy, however willing she is
to lend her body's dignity to our haste
of scribbles, freak miscalculations, waste
and slack of effort. Breda shows no surprise
when, taking five, she sees all the boundlessly
plump, footless, headless, tipsy, versions of
the self she must have dreamed she was up there,
her gesture composed of greed and pride and love.
                    She shrugs. One could have done better.

She strolls in her flowered robe toward the water fountain.
I follow her to say how much I like her gardenia.
She knew I'd noticed, and she is glad to tell how
this bloom was the first from a plant she managed to grow
from a slip so tiny a neighbor tossed it into the
alley. Just look at it now. It could bloom alone
all day at home, but to bring it to work, perhaps
would get the most . . . (doesn't say someone, despite
the rule, might see fit . . .) Her next pose clearly tips
                    her boon my way like a cocked hat.

"Every mark you make," we're warned, "had better
aspire to be specific. Don't look down
expecting your own mess to tell you whether
a something goes or not. Keep your eyes on *her;*
each line should stress commitment to *her alone.*
No belly buttons, shadows, pubic hair:
A lousy cake, with sugar frills, is still lousy!
How often do I have to tell you, *Sorta*
ain't good enough!!" For me it's not so easy,
                    with that gardenia. . . .

And maybe it's time I realized this: that
a window dresser is not the worst one could
assent to become. Am I the only one
to envy ("sorta") the model for being her own
creation, for knowing without looking, from inside,
exactly how her ankle does it with her foot.
To jut her rib just past her hip, just so,
and get it right the first time — every muscle
knowing its place — her sexy *contraposto.* . . .
                    I am not capable.

Seeing all my usual hand-heavy gestural
scribbling, cloud-head and feet (if there) afloat
in search of flooring I seem to have passed over
with less respect for grounds than for the figure,

you'd think that Breda would . . . I mean, would not
consider speaking to me, much less give subtle
assents that override what we all know is true
in art, any art, where first things first is crucial,
                    if you want to . . . & I do.

With few minutes left in this last pose I begin
to draw just what I've wanted, today, to draw
in the first place. I do not go below the neck.
I'm all on her surfaces, nape to brow to cheek,
eyelash, freckle, corkscrew and . . . gardenia,
of course. By magic, it grows, from nothing; then
seems thick as thigh, turned breast, etcetera,
as deep as solid spaces, shaped to this body
in itself, even human. . . .Time! I hand it to Breda.
                    She hands her languid gardenia to me.

$\mathcal{M}$ M

I barely learn my part. As to the whole,
I'm in the dark — excuse my dishabille —
spread thin as light. I'm really almost real,
available, for sale . . . When I took the veil

of Hollywood, of nil and la-di-da —
glittered and phosphored, hocus-pocused, glossed
with platinum tremblings, breathless, raw —
I promised nothing so much as a promise, crossed

and double-crossed my heart — that free for none
where ghosts hang on my every absence, frame
my presence, mouth my yummy name and grin —

to be a legend, Sweetheart, the cream of dreams,
sleepless . . . To do the whole scene . . .

          over and over
be taken in, exposed . . .
              you get the picture.

"JUNG AND EASILY FREUDENED": SABINA SPIELREIN'S ANALYSIS

I. Confusions (c. 1903–4): A Damp Poodle

Cramped and barren . . . No. This diary should not start so
unhopefully. Granted, this Zurich flat's low-rent,
is puny, stark; my psyche's profile, too — how
close to home! These pathological slants,

all pinched and crabby, even my handwriting
precisely suits the squeezed tight life, at heart,
in womb, out of purse. But Fridays — with Dr. Jung —
burgeon. Wide luxury, his study; his eyes my light.

My female "thrust" (he says) inspires. . . . Except I wince
to hear him try to share (too soon) insight of ours
with colleagues who shrug. His flustered hausfrau's
flinch blames me. I am willing, as well as guilty

of nonsense, mercurial provocations. Science
by reason is cryptically droned. But "Poetry"
strikes gold, "shadow-tics of Apollo's violence
deferred" (Jung's words), from near-to-ordinary

playtalk. I'm a disciple, as Jung to Freud, but more:
the Jewish daughter one might have preferred . . . to marry?
(Someone once said I resemble Matilde Freud.) Jung spores
my work. I am his star, rising above the Burgholzli

dead: ex-patient, Persephone, proof a "schizophrenic"
child who lives out whole her fairy tale, needs only
heroic hands, to lift her fingers from her eyes; to take
hold, be held. Hands, eyes. Through his she will try

and feel: how to listen, to see her meaning, to stand
herself being there. Jung himself has been "there." Found in
person a child's heartbroken babble a being bound,
a crucial story, ground to grow from. I plan. . . .

. . .

Singspiel tangles with Pangloss in Jung's den.
"Poetry": a word for talk, for sound's silver
quick ambiguities, pending. One sweet session,
more vital than all Vienna's strut. We core

peeled psyche's riddle cum rhythm, eye to pulse,
to cerebellar cadence, throb, poise, Wagner.
Jung likens his intimate friends to "a string of pearls"
selected with care for matching, weight, and luster.

He sets me apart from them, he tells me, I am
his one "medallion." I hesitate
to plumb the epic figure here; such "talk" has come
too dearly far from the ideal poetic state

we started from, to reach, contain. A heart
at work must not confuse itself with ornament,
nor gratitude with flattery, nor seedy art
with fertile secret, nor colloquy. . . . I don't

think that, say that. . . . No matter that I know
I should know better, I let his pride in me
flare up from his decked breast, unfurl in echo,
my heart beat from his. And how? Medal-lion-ally.

. . .

As soon as I take my professional degree, under Dr. Jung's
instruction of course, of course he begins to see
a certain risk. According to Freud . . . He wrongs
his charge who tongues from tip to crux each lovely

groomed finger of his masterpiece: sick hoyden
turned sanely to love. He does more when I offer
my licked hand, taking leave. . . . But then:
confused. At home, I draw my curtain closer,

undress to wash. Then see the gap . . . still wide
enough to see through, as if . . . by oversight,
this rift in modesty. . . . By accident? Belied.
I do imagine, I see this someone . . . might

be out there, darkling, prizing my eagerly young
still-new-to-me body, itself so touchingly framed
by vertical chintz folds, barely parted, pale tongue
of flesh barely visible behind. . . . Ashamed.

It was . . . a mistake. I wonder, though . . . blush, don't . . . feel
like rushing to right the breach in blind decorum
I seem to have invited. I really don't know, meanwhile,
if anyone's there. I am . . . I astonish myself. Not him.

· · ·

This Friday I was stopped at his door. "So sorry.
The Doctor is busy, just now . . . with Frau Jung in labor,
so very close, so . . . " So sorry to be. Here am I,
stray dog on a doorstep, dripping rain, dumb beggar.

I shiver, turn, cringe, go. A blessed event
indeed. Extraneous. Jung waits for his own
wife's daughter. I, too, was born one ancient
Friday, Freya's Day. I'm sworn to her. Then,

I'm running away from Her: Love, Fecundity,
Fervor, Generosity. I ask
a blessing as I turn and slip, as silly
and damp a poodle as ever braved a dusk

of thunder, broken umbrella lashed to its tail.
My skirt is torn. A flap of skin rips loose
from my left knee. Stings like any small
initial breach of closure. How very careless

one can be, on purpose, dressing against desires.
Blood uncircused leaks frail as rain. Embarrassing.
Remember Sigmund Freud. Recall how "left" declares,
in certain dreams, incest. My wound wakes pulse

to racing my heart home limp over howl to word
insofar as I can bear to . . . I do . . . barely write
this down to sleep. Forehead to knee-tuck, I shield
the shadow spread beneath me from spilled light.

II. *Sublimations (c. 1913): A Goddess Mixed with Mud*

To feel, curled under Her subtle gut-music,
the tap and probe of light, or hollow fingers
pressed into the heart — to siphon a taut excess,
or to palp it — as with breast, ripe fruit, or Bach:
this is how you know the Goddess, right from the start,
inside you, a blessed child, held in . . . with her, Art.

And this is what I knew, right from our start,
as when roused from doze by Father's huge hands,
and born aloft, as thick wind lifts, my cry made flesh
grows wings before me. Hands, roots; hurts, holds.
All bless me. Palmed hot forehead, fingered lips.
He raised me, bruised me to heal . . . relationships.

I wanted to hear what Abram got from God's lips:
"To serve, you will fly hence, leave all but transportable
needs, and those no more cumbrous than a beggar's
cupped fingers, snugged flank to flank, up to their tips,
lest a single mitzvah, talent or crumb, drop through
our nested covenant." Given. Made up as we go,

ever further from home. Tuned to promise, ego
is moving, danced, *ergo:* to give, grow . . . *up.* My small
arms part like wings, beg flight stretched from those hands
that circle my infant totter. All I could do:
to contain myself, once . . . Once, I let go . . . such a mess,
on his hands, too. I failed, I knew . . . the Goddess.

After that, *to make up was all I wanted.* Mess after mess
was all I could make. I saw: my father's hands, empty;
as usual, waiting. I'm firstborn, no son, barely good
enough to keep, feed, train. For sacrifice,
perhaps a useful substitute. I bid
my girl's hands dig as they could, down garden sod

deep hole after hole. Not for fun. I thought I should
turn up, with luck, an "other" there. A treasure
to surrender, to be, be held. I prayed: "Please grow
my hands big, fast, as Father's". I thought I would
then raise myself. I thought to slap some life
into my dolls. Father caught me. Babies come live

from Heaven, not from down here. Go wash. Live
up to our name: "*Spiel* means *play*, and *rein* means *clean.*"
How could I forget? Dirt: accident. A child
falls down, caught up, lets go . . . I will have
to make it up to him forever, his spoiled suit.
At seven, I invented alchemy. I tried to create

a fish from lint, make shit into candy, find out
God's secrets. I messed in Mother's pantry, gathered
smelly liquids, dog hairs, wax tears, leftover scraps
from the Sabbath table, dried mud, fuzz from the carpet,
moth wings. But my doll bodies, fingered to shape, refused
to breathe, or move or talk or die. Confused,

I hoarded the sad debris of self and slop inside
the dirty drum of my belly. Again and again
I'd promise the Goddess to hold on until she was ready
to come out whole and clean and in my favor.
Again and again *I'd fail*, between the pain and fault
I couldn't hide, I'd kneel spellbound, one heel tilt

tight to the betrayal-cleft. I guessed every adult,
at table especially, kept one big secret. The shame.
To know they knew ashamed me. I could look
at no one's face, nor hands, their knives and forks
that might just scoop me, or take and eat me up
and down the dank hole. I felt squeeze in every lap.

This secret would end my childhood. Where did it go —
the chewed-up mud of big guts? Would I master it
ever, myself, this vanishing's trick? — Be clean, inside
and out, light enough to fly, lifted from down below
by myself, *under my own power*, to burst with the violence
of a million words, like wings, out of the shell, *silence*

purposely shattered? To be,
                                    my Goddess, freed, to make the earth
move, right down to her bowels
                                    my own: matters of choice, birth.

III. *Consummations (c. 1920): Siegfried*

> *I say to you: one must have chaos in oneself to give birth to a
> dancing star.*
>   — Nietzsche, *Thus Spake Zarathustra*

We touched; I touched your fertile need. Had our "poetry" then
become flesh, imagine: germ of our twin souls, a pure music
fattening in me, a bridge beyond words, the rainbow end
of analysis, a newborn self. I was more than ready to bear him
out of wedlock, as Siegmund's sister bore her brother's child,
secret. Siegfried the Unborn — inconceivable? — no mere whim.

I would have taught him rudiments: to desire, and yet to shun
lust; to steal in need; to forge his sword from luckily found
father-fragments; to treasure the gold ring of transformation
and the hero's Tarnhelm, given by Nature . . . to understand
the dues and duties, the language . . . instinct, murder, love.
To be ready to die. To unravel this, this child I had in mind,

has taken me all of my life. Interlocutor, minstrel to my madness
maybe, the thought of him led to . . . acts more than just theatrical.
I wonder if Abraham felt something similar: under orders to sacrifice
not only himself, but his child, his life's one best possession?
Is betrayability the same as love one lives for?
Are beginnings of insight a gift? Blank passion? No question

is higher, more deeply felt. Only the fruitful dare
to destroy as much as I, to care. By surprise,
your words, last time, took me. I kissed your ear
despite an edgy fidget. How your paper knife seized my left
hand, suddenly . . . You grab, shout. How? "You struck me!"
Did I? Impossible to grasp . . . I go blank, blind, deaf.

I come to, later, weeping. In a filthy Zurich trolley,
hands over eyes. "Look!" someone says, "she's injured!"
I look. My left wrist, forearm . . . Bloody. "It's not," I cry,
"my blood, it's his. I *murdered him!*" Whispers; I'm alone.
At home, I wash, and probe the stigmatoid
parentheses round my wrists impressed by your ten

slick nails. Our struggle's unrecalled signature . . . detail?
Overcome? I came to confess. But what? To whom?
Freud's image surged up between us, a sort of angel
of parcel delivery. I sat down, wrote Freud a poem,
a letter about Siegfried; and you, of course; and the mess
you'd made of us. I calmed. Then, Freud's answer came.

His question: What did I expect? How had I dared what I did?
He had such concern for you, remember? You, his errant, Aryan son.
And as for me: I was, as you'll guess, hardly comforted.
You men stick tight, you *Doktors*. Who in the world am *I*
to complicate your bond? A naughty, little, girl, hysteric.
So I headed straight for Vienna: The Only Way

I could see to end chagrin, deliver our Siegfried
up, in person; I'd tender my dream to the spooked Old Man
in His inner sanctum. I'd be doused with gospel, hear said:
"You express, Fraulein, naught but the commonest type
of fantasy known to Analysis." Thus did Freud
start mucking out the Child from my manger of sleep.

Come clean at last, I married. "Siegfried" was no more
than a put-away toy, a childish, undignified shame.
So I thought, foresaw nothing. I was starting over,
caught up in career. I see now how the lives we give
our first loves to, in poetry or in rings of fire, must refuse
to be so easily refused. They lie in wait, to return, to live

themselves out in us, to their proper ends. "Siegfried" found me
once more, in extremity, a fresh ring of fire, my daughter
about to be born. I felt them struggle, a deadly
battle to one's birth. My daughter, finally, won.
Renate: reborn. I named her for how I know she fought
her brother inside, his gold brawn never known

except (by her) in the dark she fought to leave
behind in me. She brings the stolen cap of darkness.
The Tarnhelm, worn, translates all animal babbles — grief
to joy created, grunted; whistled, plotted. I put on
the gold ring that likewise she brought me. Relation
granted. Myth no less binding, bound. . . . I listen

each day now, to the baby's early bird-sounds, and my daily piano
practice fills the house I keep. At last, I understand. *Spielrein:*
plays clean, sublime; plays. All masters flow
from my fingers, white keys, black keys. Music
expands all my life contracted. Once. All day I ponder:
No single act, dream. . . . My thoughts turn, not sorry, hermetic:

We are gladioli, drunk from wet soil, sword-lilies guilty
and pure, re-forged from found father-shards, gleaned
eloquent as any Goddess' wounds. Love: radiantly
criminal growth through chaos . . . continued, all, part,
transformed Siegfried finally. Sage fingers tap
my heart, invisibly pierce, lift, gorge each rapt room

of mine as if a female Abraham were about to . . .
                              to rocket up from Bethlehem.

$\mathcal{M}$ISS AMERICA
COMES ACROSS HER DAUGHTER

for my mother

Plans

There you are at the three-way mirror, the same
mirror I grew up in, checking left and right
profiles against each other . . .

On the one hand you see beauty, on the other beast;
and straight ahead, in plain view of the wall
and door behind you,

I stand, spied and spying on you as you make up
a not original daydream palaver, lips closing
round that kissable "no."

My reflector, my inquisitor, together you and I
are a much of a muchness, a symmetry
of symmetries

and inner mysteries, oracles and fairy tales,
and from Nancy Drew to Madison Avenue —
copies and copies sold —

retold. You are my living doll; I make you
all over in my image, teach you how to:
cross your ankles,

sit tight with a tiny teacup on your knee; play
fair at hopscotch, dibs, and Sunday school
picnics; eschew hangnails,

use lipstick, white lies, charm, and embroidery;
be well-dissembled in the eyes of the fathers;
posture, posture . . .

I've been here before. I kissed the first words
into your mouth: please and thank you, no
and thank you, please . . .

To get on, Miss America must know thresholds,
how to urge an entranceway out of thin air,
She must smile

at the perfect pitch-dark, as if unblinded by the glare.
Greet the blankness warmly, like an old old friend.
Talent? Well, it's true

you never learned to sing or dance or play the accordion,
to paint a face that wasn't yours, yodel, prestidigitate . . .
but you might do

a speech on how to pack a picnic hamper, or recite
"The Spider and the Fly." Or dress as
Betsy Ross and whistle

"The Stars and Stripes" on roller skates. In three minutes
you have to come across as something special,
but not too serious.

Lessons

It sounds so easy. Mother may I? Step-hop-jump?
No, you may not. Glide this way in baby steps
as queens must do

in swimsuit and evening gown. See how I walk on air,
twinkletoe by, disguise the fact that the human gait is a chain
of interrupted falls . . .

That's it, and then you catch yourself up on your toes,
brush knee over knee to smooth the uncouth bounce,
eliminate all space

between your thighs, and, presto! — you're a mermaid
on a unicycle. Be sure to think of bubbles,
diamonds, Tinkerbell

and poodle puppies. Your eyes must be the exclamation points
on every utterance, your lips slide like electric doors
over your well-greased teeth.

Impress your life on your judges. Tell them
Daniel Boone and Pocahontas hang
in your family tree.

I said that I watered my prize-winning 4-H turnips
with vodka and grape pop, that I began to be pretty
when I began reciting

the Lord's Prayer in the tub. Anything you say is true
enough. And they'll begin to see Her in you —
only She — no me, no you.

Promises

Now, how glad you must be I made you slave
in beauty's Siberia from twelve to seventeen, live
the loser-to-looker cliché

that made me, crowned me half my life ago,
your superlative average Miss America:
five foot six

one hundred and eighteen thirty-five twenty-three
thirty-four golden hair blue eyes
that have seen the glory;

engaged in unrelenting search from alligator
farms to war zones, from country
fairs to teamsters'

conventions, singing "God Bless America," launching
Mickey Mouse balloons, kissing tame bears;
the little engine

that could, and did. And now, by the mother-daughter-
holy ghost of poise, by diet and deep knee bend
will you also worship

our shape of success, the hourglass figure with its three minutes
of talent, and all the fairy tales will fall
right into place

behind you, shining white pebbles to show you home.

*T*HE WIVES OF WATERGATE

for my father

I don't know what happened. I am just telling you what every-
body thinks happened, what might have happened, what you are
saying happened. If that is history, I am telling you history.
— Rose Mary Woods

The Account: Martha Mitchell

No, I didn't want to go to town
like we did . . . for God knows what . . . election.
But then, there were the perks and parties thrown
for us, and how many gals have the FBI
around to iron their gowns and zip them up?
One day I marched with the Salvation Army.
I organized the Cabinet wives and cut down
those dumb old oaks so John could have a longer
view from the Attorney General's office. I hope
I improved things, and then of course I had to
say what I thought, and I thought truth was stronger
than protocol. John called me his unguided
missile. I told the press John was my favorite hero
in all history. I let my mouth go to my head.
But I'll have you know my heart was in it too.

I'm from the South and marriage is more important
to me than politics. Let me let you in
on a secret: Richard Nixon stole my husband,
warped his ear and heart. It wasn't any fun
anymore to be wife of the top cop in the game.
There was a fishy fume in Washington.

I speak the truth and they put it out I'm a lush.
They want me to climb up the wall. O.K. —
but only as far as the writing on it. I see
what I see and I say what I saw. I am so
sick of being pitied — and she said Martha's
"sick," but no flowers came as far as I know.
It's not menopause. I'm going to watch the news:
I want to know how long I'm going to be
a political prisoner. When I am free
I'm going to write a book. My elephant memory
is already on tape, and let me tell you, Honey,
there will be no (expletive deleted)
secrets about those suitcases of boodle
sitting in my hall, or the way I've been treated
or Richard Nixon's . . . (unintelligible) . . .
I'm going to bring the house down, speak my mind.
It's going to sell better than *Gone with the Wind.*

I'm telling you: I am important enough
to be killed. I've waked up screaming for how
many years now . . . ? The little girl from Pine Bluff . . .

I've waked up screaming ever since California,
ever since the CREEP that I believed in
broke into the Watergate. We got the alert
at 6:30 A.M. And that was when
everything was decided. I was going to get hurt.

Up 'til then John thought my honesty
was real cute, and King Richard even said
"Give 'em hell, Martha." They'd given me
so much of it, I had it to give. Instead
of thanks, they lock me up with thugs, wrestle
the telephone out of my hands, beat me up,

stick a needle in my ass, go and tell
the world I'm a boozer, and a loon — no hope
for Martha. Well, Martha's got her bathroom
phone, eyes, and a tongue. Has her reason.
It was filthy politics and not my man
I wanted my separation from.

Sweetheart, I'm up salt crick,
and if I'm sloshed, well, I have a reason to be:
they are trying to put me away, they open my mail,
my telephones click and pop, they killed Allende,
and they can do the same to me what with all
their Mafia buddies. Listen, if you don't hear
from me, you have them drag the East River.

That's right. I threw his goddamn clothes
right out in the hall. Then I got on the phone,
but I don't recall who I called — sometimes
I think maybe the fake Martha — you know, the one
who makes these calls and gives my name —
is me after all. Who else would be so stupid,
so hurt — I swear — I tell myself you're
wrong, Martha. I say it hasn't happened

to you. You are dreaming it, Martha. What
I want is to be in Pine Bluff in a grave
alongside my mother, my mother who never gave
a damn. It's come to that. This is the end.
No more. I'm signing off. I don't need it.

The play's the thing: Pat Nixon

I met Richard Nixon at a play
audition — the parts we wanted I forget.
He was showing off. He caught my eye,
but I . . .
        I thought he was some kind of nut.

He hung around. I fixed my roommate up
with him. That didn't work. And he would drive
me to Los Angeles, all patter and pep,
for my dates with other men —
                         indicative
of great persistence, if not passion. Well.
It got to me — his single-mindedness.

Apart from me — I saw — the fugitive goal
inspired the play, and his weird . . .
           stick-to-itiveness? . . .
moved me finally.
          I chipped in to buy
the engagement ring. I wanted a family.

One day some guy from the Republican Party
called up. I don't know why they thought of Dick.
It was for him . . . I guess . . . I don't quite know . . .
like a play or kind of courtship, and all's fair
in love and . . . I was in love and even though
I'd been hoarding for a house . . . before

I could say "knife" our house became the House
and our life one long long run. I've been both staff
and distaff. I tire, but I never cancel out.
I go on. Sometimes I even laugh

at the way things conspire. I'm glum sometimes.
I think the greatest luxury would be
to frown for one whole day and not
touch another person, just one whole day
of anonymity . . .
                    free time for who knows what.

Once, in '54, I had an evening
all for myself. Could not think what I ought
to do (Dick had gone off to do something
secret), so I pressed every single suit
in his closet.
                  I guess you'll laugh at that scene.
I just hate complainers. I won't complain.
Don't come to me now and ask about Watergate.
. . . it's politics and it will go away. I pray. I will myself
not to be afraid or sick or bored.
I will myself to love, and I do. The wolf
is at the door, but it's an imperfect world,

so what do you want me to say? I keep right on
answering letters. Thousands. I read each one.

I answer, not for everyone, but as I can.
The play has dulled me. But I still go on.

Saving history: Rose Mary Woods

Secretaries need their sleep as much
as anyone. They need to dream they'll meet
The Man on His Way, indispensably attach
themselves to power. This is, of course, just what

happened to me. There was, as everybody
knows, an incident in '52.
All our lives were turning topsy-turvy.
I stood with Pat. I had a cloth coat, too.

I helped her with the kids. I fed the dog
most likely to change the world. And in my hand
I held the telegram to Ike — the big
gesture: resignation. Would I send

it? I would have sooner strangled Checkers.
I held on. I had hold of both our futures.

Ike liked Dick's show. Before Dick knew, he cried
backstage. He cried to me and not to Pat.
I joked with him. Just sleep on it, I said.
He did. Our dreams got bigger after that,

despite hurled stones in Caracas, the dirty
race of 1960, when such a lot
of dead Democrats were resurrected by
machine to vote for Mr. Camelot,

despite the loss of California's
governorship, and tears again, and years

in between when I and I alone was
his whole staff to comfort him, holding
on . . . We were sleeping on it, gathering
the affluent majority in *their* nightmares.

I moved up as my man moved. I even
got my suite in the Watergate, and clothes
that sparkle. I have a million mementos,
doodads worth a break-in, finally. Heavens!

I am the one he doesn't have to finish
his sentences for. But now I don't know what
to do . . . these transcripts . . . how to save the face
behind them. I don't recall why I should type it
exactly so . . .

                                All day with this damn earphone,
trying to put straight this patchiness
of static, whisper, expletive, and hiss . . .
This is what it's come to? Said and done?

Eighteen minutes of my typing life.
Eighteen minutes in the Oval Office.
Eighteen minutes. I have had enough.
What is eighteen minutes, more or less?

I don't know what happened. I am just
telling you. I must have been half-asleep.
I didn't want a single word to get lost.
So much noise over it. What I wouldn't give
for even more silence. It was a slip.
I swear. It's gone — what I tried to save.

Sugar and spice and everything: Tricia Nixon Cox

I do not unnecessarily smile.
I do not care to. In '68 I did
my bit. For instance, I agreed to preside
over Virginia's Azalea Festival.

(We were so scared the election would be stolen
from him the way it was in 1960.
Those evil people have always hated Daddy.
They call me the tiniest Nixon, the careful one.)

But there I was, strep throat on top of it all,
keeping going by knowing how my father
would stop the violence and all the juvenile
delinquency, remembering how to flatter:
"Oh, I just love your azaleas! Oh, I love
that birdcage! All that silver — just imagine
polishing it!" I was beside myself,
pouring out the sugar and spice, and then . . .
    WE WON.
But the campaigns are never never over.
Even after we were in the White House
I was supposed to get up early, care
about schools, mental hospitals, ghettos,
go out and show it. I did give a masked ball
I cared about. And that was about all.

He ordered it — seven feet of wedding cake —
for my Big Day in the world, in the Rose Garden.
I'd like to spend my life dashing that way
through flower petals to the waiting limousine,
knowing he is smiling just for me. I'd like
to be a perfect child again, smile naturally.

Then I had my own home and my china,
Blue Tree by Lennox, and Lunt's Eloquence
for silver. For a while the media
were just interested in me for slants
on young marrieds. "Love is the most important
thing," I say, "but love is so intangible."
They nod. "Cooking's arcane," I say, "I can't
do bacon just right, but I suppose I will
learn." Now there is this Watergate caper.
Humiliation never ends. Accusers everywhere!
My Dresden figurines. The practiced smile.
Always in danger. Somehow I knew the evil
would win. *To grow up is a real disaster.*

A caution: Katharine Graham

How did I get my power, such as it is?
I started out with everything but love.
A spoiled childhood. Where there is money enough
to go around, but hardly a goodnight kiss,
you learn . . . to look before, to test the wind,
let sleeping dogs, . . . to see, to feel, to count
the cost . . . caution and toughness are what you want.
Don't hear your mother's praise: "Dear, you remind
me of myself." Just turn away. I learned
my father's work. I faced the empty page
and bit my lip 'til words came, and rage
at emptiness filled out some profile, sound
or not. A story done. With vultures all
around, to give up is unthinkable.

Obviously, you won't risk your whole
newspaper if you don't think that you have
something worth it. I always said that all
we were doing was a piece of investigative
reporting. There isn't any other motive.
I let some risky things go to press, but hell,
anybody who's imaginative
could have seen the writing on the wall,
at least after Woodward and Bernstein's oracle
started to spout from the deep source, to give
so much that checked out. Those three were the brave
ones. All I did was realize in full
this story that was happening, was real.
If I suffered, I suffered to believe.

I prefer to keep my opinions to myself.
(For years I was a no-opinion person.)
We're not, at the *Washington Post*, goddamn
it, do-gooders! We're not the big bad wolf.

Watergate? I'll tell you what it means
to me: a good story, a specific play
of specific characters. It is not the way
everything is. You don't, in the end,
tell any definitive Truth when neutrality
is your god. The awful magnitude
uncovered is no more than a prelude.
Then reflections, for each alone. Reality
is all we hope to bring to light. And after all,
it's not a moral business, not political.

QUEEN CHARMING
WRITES AGAIN

for Alice, yet another revision

> *A woman writing thinks back through her mothers.*
> — Virginia Woolf

Dear Godmother,
　　　　　　Another year, and today
Charmingshire's Serendipity Rendezvous
Ball rolls round again, with all my festive duties
of gratitude; thus, my annual letter to you.
I wish you could see the gorgeous pumpkin taxi

I've ordered for my Good Will Progress (dim
patch, though stable, on your conjured coupe). I'll visit
the village, street hovel I once called home.
The house has its blue plaque now. I remember it
as "modest," but now it's disgraceful — a slum!

I guess the present tenants dress in rags and smear
their faces with soot just to try to catch *my* eye,
as if a mere grubby urchin caught yours! I'm sure
all year they're as clean, neat, and happy as everybody
back then but me. I was more than your lazy beggar,

I'd like to shout. I was a *real* princess at heart.
Can I tell them they have to do more than mope
for *my* money? Can't the luckless do more than look hurt?
How vile, this charity business! There's no glib escape,
I'd like to tell them: learn to pander, stoop to flirt.

And yet, as I muse on going back, the twitchy
footmice and Pega-soused rats you reorganized
for my swell-cum-clodpate courtship pageantry
debut still run loose and wild in my galvanized
pasture of nightmares. I wonder: Why do they

have more reality than the King? Don't tell
me you're just reminding me how much I owe
to your clout behind the scenes. Your pure goodwill
I can't quite believe in anymore. So what if now
I just said "no!": A rotten job, being royal.

Would I get my own back? Would I look like *them?*
Or would I indulge in the same old song and dance,
only, this time around, to lose? The snickers come
like flocks of moths at night. No daily circumstance
compares, bears thinking of . . . Yet, I grow numb

with satisfactions. Do many of your pets
come back asking for trouble like this, or am I
doomed to the unforgivable peeves and snits
of my not-I underclass? Where is the charity
of your original senses, of humor and limit?

Have I mislaid so much? My maiden nickname
still flutters in the dark, scantling, recherché,
whisking and shushing — its tatty, ashen rhythm
around my heart, still driven to the tune of seedy
axles, fare-meter's click-cluck time; about time . . .

But come morning, my royal pseudo- (or is it alter-?)
nym comes back to me, to stir me from my tangled bed.
I wake, and see reverted Pumpkin take to the air
in streaks of distant reflection, distant cloud.
I hear the King's footsteps, and then his tap at my door.

He brings a breakfast tray — such a sweetie, really.
I have nothing to complain of there, unless
of his unremitting kindness, an idiotic, saintly
charm binding me to our secret undeservingness.
I wiggle my toes, still almost numb from my crazy

nightlong jigging in your hallucinatorium.
They feel half-slippered still, one see-through strap
of solid tears wearing thin. I kick to free them
for the daily round, prosaic as my shining cup
of tea. I pour a steady, miraculous stream

of glitters, strained to absolute clarity,
golden as silence, hospitable to cloud. Lemon
or milk? I stare into the cup, past the glimmery
ghost's breath on the surface . . . Mother? . . . Gone.
The King bends to kiss me good-morning. "Silly,"

he whispers, "time to rise and shine, drink up before
it's cold. We've got a big day ahead of us."
Oh, yes, the flowers, the pastries, last-minute palaver
and fidgets over the guest list . . . And so I dress,
put on my manners, my face, my workaday collar

and coronet. I check my regalia, pressed and hung straight
for the evening's do. All day I'm Queen, charming to boot,
but even on such a royal day, as you know . . . midnight
strikes me hard, dumps my brain right back in the ashbucket,
glad rags and all. But of course you know. You wait

at the garden hedge, call softly . . . We happen all over
again. I swallow my doubts and fetch an unlikely
squash. I watch my sooty creep-mouse pinafore
dissolve, revise, riddle over with a finery
to equal my envy. I see mice evolve to power,

each tiny hack capacity harnessed somehow
under your wand. Everything you do to disguise
me, right down to the oddity of the transparent shoe,
is supposed to make me more or less myself, I guess.
But which? Without the punctual nightmare, could the show

go on? Could you take it from me? Could you let me stop
the rehearsals — sorting the lentils from ashes, my guilty
visits to the hazelnut tree, to keep
the crooked breeze green by Mother's grave? Will I
forever fall for Narcissus' echo, clap-

trappedly snapping up rejection to re-cinder
my nest? Do you keep me at this to improve
my character, or intend to turn your back-burner
simmer down to silence soon? Please forgive
my confusion — bad enough to need another

spectacular rescue, but not deserve the same.
My wonder ripens, despite the years of cool satin.
The windfall, the sunrise reprieve does come
to some felons convicted, even she who's done in
the child she was expecting . . . to be . . . This is as

(unclear — I'm sorry — *but you know what I mean* —

if anyone could.) Do our humiliating pangs
of separation ever soften? Today, We hold an audience,
The King and I, for all our subjects — their hopes, harangues,
tragic or funny stories — noblesse oblige! — each grievance
attended, assuaged. And *then*, of course, the flings

and curtsies of the dance. Have you scoured the countryside
for someone my grown son might see fit to marry?
He's ready, and if she works out, I shall take her aside
and promise her no change but constancy's. . . .
She'll know I'm a witch, your opposite, and need

to regard me, if at all, as I did my own stepmother,
bless her hearth. Let's hope for one who wants not
to change the world too loudly. Someday let her
enjoy her babies and fêtes, write you a thank-you note
as pleasing as should be, more than I can muster.

All who chance to enter into the state of Charming,
I'd tell her, are charged with a possible grace,
a tentative keeping — of promise, houses, time
and with luck, a sense of humor, figure, face
that can fall and lift again, to pray or scream . . .

As never, ever,

Your "Cinderella"

GROSS PRELUDE: SAID AND DONE

for Maurice

1. *A happiness*

"Your heart sounds fine," Susanne, the midwife said:
"A tiny murmur, the beat's last half split slightly —
in pregnancy that's normal . . . to be expected . . .
I'd guess eight weeks," she said, as she fingered, inside me,
that lode whose gist I sensed remotely, at best:

> a speck pulling strings, clandestinely attached —
> to vagus nerves, lush aches in my hitherto tiny
> breasts, a ligament's sudden flex, its hammock stretched
> to this side or that, curved needle stitching close
> to the bone parenthesis of an iliac crest.

> I sense it by pluck, by the fact I feel at ease,
> so otherly happy, and happier, having pinched this one
> small germ from chaos, conferring its diocese,
> than ever I've felt, over anything witful I've done.

2. *Happenstance*

"Some cramps, some staining, can happen, around the day
you'd have had a period," my midwife said.
"It's normal, in early pregnancy . . . in, say, forty
percent . . . Some doctors will send you straight to bed —
to minimize guilt, that's all — if anything should
go wrong. So, not to worry. Nothing you do
right now would influence what normally would
miscarry in any case. Relax. But *do*
call if the stain *should* turn bright red; take two
Tylenol, nothing stronger, for the pain."

I did what she said, and I entertained a friend
for dinner. The pain increased, and in the end
bright red replaced the stain, came bursting through
its knot. I lay forehead to knee,

> and *this thing was done.*

3. *Hearts and flowers*

Friday, the Thirteenth: it happens tomorrow is
St. Valentine's Day. It may not be appropriate
to see so much . . . I mean, so much blood, with roses —
a dozen, long-stemmed, still to open, coming out
regardless, so blooming, and just . . . so cut,
each one, from its root, just so . . . so *given.* Is
their show any less appropriate, given that
hearts bleed, and not mine singly, mine that rose
to beat, to the occasion of another . . . 'til now
almost . . . down there, in here . . . that sown there by
the lover who placed, in this fragile vase, these roses,
to breathe as they might, above us, where I lie
delivered of a heart. Yesterday was . . . tomorrow
too, once; apropos, we see so much — still — to bless us.

4. *What remains*

I'd always wondered how a person could believe
against all evidence, in the Reverend Moon
and that ilk; and then, as quickly reverse and shun
conversion. I have a clue now, now that I grieve
for pregnancy, as unlikely, as suddenly lost
as faith, and as painfully. So there, then so gone:

one cannot believe one believed, or that the brain
could be so full of the invisible body, then be washed,
and so quickly, clean of that blood, that never was
meant to go on, to hold that world of promise,

continued purpose, borne, created by
our wish for it to be. Left in Pandora's
box of evils, I recall, was the delusion
of hope, not hope itself, but no less of joy.

5. quis separabit

I don't know what to do with this sadness, this
hard nothing where something was — I don't know what.

There was little heart, yet my heart went out to that,
as much, all, as if there were meant to be two of us
in this one boat. How hard, to separate
that issue of blood from this, this one that continues
along the selfsame veins that gave . . . that happiness
its core, presentiment, its fantasy set —

like figures on a wedding cake, and no more real
than that; yet meaningful. So sugars abandon
the tongue, make nothing easier to swallow,
                    the taste having gone, and so quickly too . . . after all,

"I do" is never over, but an act to follow
with another, and nothing should need to be . . . undone.

6. *Museum piece*

I'm not asking for time to heal this wound,
or even for time to leave me its visible scar,
an X, say, where a treasure might yet be found,
dug up, in memory or prospect, for gossips or
curators to assess, imagine in place.

Some place of their knowledge? Certainly the power,
or question, of fortune lost — to integrities
of body, psyche, tribe — should not demur
to healing, by time or by any means at all.

My knowledge, carnal, is still, is cured with salt
in part, an open secret, yet invisible;

an inexpensive cure,   yet paid to a fault —
in spirit, in full —

                    the cost irrational.

So nearly nothing may come to nothing — material —
yet net a gain — and much in the way of knowledge . . .
                    in fact, all.

PSYCHE'S SUITE

$Prelude:$ Lusus Naturae*

I. THE MOTHER OF BEAUTY AND THE KING

$She:$

> How could I guess a world's collective breath
> would be so taken, in and away, at mere sight of her?
> or revel in beauty made to carry her air of death
> so carelessly?
> > So did I dream, a mother-
> to-be, of prodigies and monsters? Of course. Afraid,
> I hoped against hope, presumed against all odds,
> near-mother-wise, that this pip at sea in me
> would cruise to term, nurse, grow . . .
> > > > Of course I prayed.

$He:$

> My mortal countenance, "King," rendered over and over —
> $in\ specie,$ signet, portrait, parchment, what-have-you —
> confers my face value, sweet as pie. But my daughter . . .

$She:$

> Our Princess appeared. So fragile, I named her Psyche.

$He:$

> The young men come, adore, stare, and will not woo.
> For fear . . . ? (That's what I hear.) Is she not mortal?
> And as I am . . .

---

* $lusus\ naturae$ = "sport of nature," monster, marvel.

She:

> There at her window, she's framed for all to see.
> Jittery and suave as aspic, her blood's as cool
> as a tadpole's tongue and by all accounts as un-
> accountable.

He:

> As King and Father, I'd ban . . .
> But whose trick is this? Did one of that swell
> Oympian bunch need such a spanking new
> fresh mortal breath? Why ours?

She:

> Word spreads: "unearthly,"
> a "something else" . . . "to believe, you must go and see . . . "

He:

> They say now they'll kill me if I try to hide her,
> our so-called uncalled-for "light of the world" . . . Aphrodite!

She:

> Why fan Aphrodite's stale old flames? Who needs our
> fluke mongrel luck? This dainty, empty shell,
> our Psyche; or beastly goddess . . .

He:

> . . . to whom no mother
> can offer a mortal hope, nor hold a candle:

She:

> dim bulb as I first knew her to be, and know
> her still, to be, inside . . .

He:

> I wanted no *lusus naturae,*
> nor the world to wonder. . . .

She:

She *is,* though. They *do.*
For that, the King will scarcely look at me.

2. APHRODITE MAKES WAVES

It's true, I have not cared to show my face
or hand in this Psyche affair; nor my disgust
with mortal rivalry and vogues — this arriviste
cult doll particularly! I've ordered Eros,
dear blinkered boy, to deal with the Psyche fad.
He's trained to break new waves, to turn them into
old firm-crest nags. I want Psyche driven mad,
hitched to some beastly cripple or gigolo —
disgraced, in short. Unbearable virgin! Discarnate
monster! I? The resonant waves that bore me
espouse me still. Where air and water meet
and mount

> *in sympathetic loops, I delve my way*
> *toward shore; against her shallow chafe, each molecule*
> *of my being slows, each orbit flattens, hauled from the great*
> *searoot of speed and depth 'til my pinched crests curl,*
> *foam, heave, break hard over air, and*
>   *as suddenly . . .*
> *suck down, lull, settle back.*
>   *All waves behave*
> *according to this form — so does madness, noise,*
> *love, childbirth, the current rage — my own and only*

Beauty's law. Psyche bows under Aphrodite;
Eros kneels to a maternal wink. Now get this
straight, you mortal stargazers: Psyche's out! —

> *out of sight, luck, mind, her tinsel a long shot*
> *from Heaven, me or mine. No mortal takes place*
> *at my heights or depths; I issue the way I do*

for pleasure, moreover; it thrills me stretching out
to broaden, swell, for myself to ripen, rush
drawn headlong out from a long-winded fetch . . .

demand my due.

Stupor Mundi

1. MORTAL QUESTIONS

The Queen:

Had I any hope, presentiment, or scheme
against the gods, with Psyche in my womb?
Or guess my casual embryo might assume
remarkable alchemies? Did I fake arcane

prenatal inklings, freak euphoria?
Before (or after) the worm of her conception
began to show, could I put my finger on
some telltale omen, symptom, insignia?

a star-shaped mole? ectopic twinge? Did my belly
rise more demurely, rounder, closer to my heart?
Did my bones tell, or haruspex spill, or Delphi?

Who was my midwife? Did I use a witch's art,
spells, ointments? sell my soul to Persephone?

No, no, no. Though it *would* make a better story . . .

2. BIG DEAL

The King:

What can Psyche's father do? My castle
no longer my home, but Psyche's shrine.

Poor prize,
showpiece! She mopes, oppressively visible,
her beauty unasked for, her wrath-of-god rivals
no fault of her own.

                                                    Nor mine.
                                              I fear Psyche is —
like recherché objets d'art, a cult pet, idol —
as good (to tell the truth) as dead. I know this
sounds hard. I hate to say it. But something will

soon *have* to be done, if only to keep the peace,
to keep our grounds from being trashed by tourists,
shills, gawkers, souvenir stands. I sent for
                                      Delphi's
advice, my last resort: Psyche *must* wed,
the oracle says.
                    Yet only a "Power of Darkness"
can fill the bill.
                    Expose her, let her be
swept up by storm from the mountain's top; you'll see
her mantled with dragon-seed, unwed from her good
girl grief. The details need not spoil the prospect of
a holiday to remember.
                                      Always. With Love.

3. IN MEMORIAM

    — Despite our trimmings, in the end, she looked a fright.
        — Left wedged that way in the folds of that crater-crag.
    — An unstrung puppet.
                        — Empty as a sucked goose egg.

    — Then the storm goes blasting at the dome of night,
and cracks its black glass beetle husk.
                                      — Its thunder
romps off in waves like drums and a trumpet.
    — A million elephants rutting.
                              — All for our sister . . .
    — Her lively, once, as a footstool.
                              — Fetched up as straight
as hellbent lace, folderol.

— Her eyes,
transparent dark grapes . . .

       — With splinters poking out
like diamond shrapnel.

       — Her face pale, dumb goat cheese . . .
— A moonstruck doorknob.

       — Why brood . . . — Tricky bait
for Aphrodite's dog.

       — Or owl-winged lizard, maybe . . .
— Horns and feet, hands full of arrows . . .

       — Scummy
snake's tail.

       — Sweet Sis, let's not get carried away . . .
— No, no more gross assumptions.

       — The trudge back down
was rather dreary, after all . . .

       — So sodden, groggy.

— After birth-labor's done, they say, you're too undone
to care for a midwife's ovation.

       — Much less the child's cry.

4. BEYOND MIDWIFERY, ANON

A pin through a butterfly's heart: will chemistry
or art explain the pathological plan,
a Psyche's stake in being a would-be none-
such creeping to crawl an epic path? Is she

a part or our whole point? She scrawls her dank-
lipped signature, bite by bite, through plush and sour-
veined milkweed — haphazard business, bitter blank
graphed marrow, identity . . .

       Whom the thinnest air
will brush, blood wash, muse fire, and shore sand down:

grim ripple, nub end, unself-
                      satisfying

she's nabbed the wave "far out" — in the nick of wings,
step-strokes to ride the given grain between
whatever hells —   just happening.

As if forever gently spread, exact, worth pain.

5. THE SISTERS WITNESS

   — So what did you think of *that* spectacle?
                            — It made
me sick, to tell you the truth.
                      — Next to Psyche's fête
our own weddings might have been funerals.
                            — Too bad
her good-bye gown went with her . . .
                            — Enough wispy
silk to swathe us two like Aphrodite's
elect. . . .
                      — Did you ever see a black organdy
as colorful?
                      — A witch must have spun such gloss . . .

   — No, the midwife's spiders did it. So she told Mother.
They started work the day that Psyche was born.

   — Oh, really! Such crazy hag notions!
                            — The whole thing reeks.
   — Witch-garbage.
                      — Hexed, if you ask me, sewn under
a wet moon.
              — Drippy as Psyche.
                            — Oh, these freaks. . . .
   — Her twinkletoe boots? Why mourn . . .
                            — The diadem?
                                  — Just forget her!

Cupid's Scherzo

1. A FINE AND PRIVATE PLACE

Psyche wakes to discover she's been taken,
body and soul, from one fatal predicament

to this one:
     Hell's premises? She wonders. High-rent,
a palace, inner courts with boastful tokens
of savvy arts, old glitz. Was it not in vain, then —
her being given up?
       What weird enchantment!
To be trusted?
      Sweet voices answer. Food, then wine,
as if from nowhere, touching lights and music . . .
God-given?
    Oh, surely: the equipage divine
of brimming privacy. But should she? — take
this in without punishment? So far . . .

       Why would
she mourn a world and family who so kindly
set up to celebrate, parade her death-day?
Could Psyche live with this?
       Yes, Psyche could.

2. SOME NOT QUITE ENCHANTED EVENINGS

Soon, something funny started up at night.
A voice, as if embodied; a touch, almost
of flesh, yes, flesh, but silkier . . . Her sight
was foiled by darkness only. Her ghost, her guest,
her host, whoever this was, left her confused

before daybreak could clear her conscience up. . . .

— Did you not feel just a little twinge of pity?

　　　— A bit, perhaps, but mixed. It's hard to judge
　　a sacrifice so laced with privilege.

— You don't mean, surely, you still might envy Psyche
her being scooped, sucked up that way, as if guilty . . .

　　　— If she'd been kind — less willing to engage
　　in nothing, less glued to her high chair, sickly image . . .

— She should have laughed off that goddess business — really!

— It wasn't funny.
　　　　　　　　　— Dumb Bunny, we called her, Miss Fitt.
— If she *is* what Delphi said . . .
　　　　　　　　　　— She'll land on her feet.
— She was too much with us, now gone . . .
　　　　　　　　　　— I'm bored to tears
already.
　　　　— We've got our husbands.
　　　　　　　　　　— Better a blind date
with dragons than sit here crying . . .
　　　　　　　　　　— Let's keep our ears . . .
— Eyes open. . .
　　　　　— Lots better than drool on an empty plate.

4. . . . CONTINUED

Psyche'd been told she'd wake up married. Maybe.
Weird nights. Invisible days. Her pride was shot.
No daylight husband. She knows she should not be
so happy. So far as fingers "see" she thought
a "someone" knelt, touched back . . .

And then, one day,
her sisters are at the door.

"You dope!" they say.

As if she had not died   *"Why can't you see?"*
for this . . .

So much is clear. So much is not.

5. SISTERHOOD

Where did *they* come from all of a sudden? *Why?*
She'd been so glad — without their creepy peephole
envy, advice, all they stood for — for waning worldly
relations, her whole premortal dream and ball
of wax — gone.

How had they found her out? Why now?
Yes, Psyche was queasy . . . alone, yes . . . and perchance
with child?

When Psyche'd been virgin, hopeless (though
deified), these two were distant. Pleased to dance
at Psyche's funeral.

Do sisters smell
a cryptic difference?

Had she come alive once more,
with child?

Apart from her humanity,
Psyche'd been happy.

"But you have to know who you are
in bed with," they said.

"The father, who is he?"

("Look," they said,

"in the dark, you can never tell.")

6. MIDNIGHT OIL

"— So listen, this is what you'll have to do,"
they said. " — You take this lamp and hide it under
a blanket beside your bed, and when you're sure
he's sleeping, look. And if what we think is true
is true, you'll have this knife. Here, under your pillow.
You wimp, just do what we say. Do you hear?"

                                And later —

She heard — his breath and heartbeat, slow — uncovered
her lamp, forbidden, and studied in its glow
no scaly monster, but this hunk of her dreams:
                                  this god.
Her hand shook; she sloshed a drop of the scalding oil.
His shoulder sparkled like a dove's neck. He woke to gleam;
her knife's edge threw him; " — I'm going home," he said,
"to Mother, if she'll have me. Follow? We're done
for . . . Love? No!"
                    Just fascination . . . forbidden.

Panic Fugue

I. PAN'S TRICK

With Eros gone, nothing to lose, no plan
in mind, Psyche tried to drown herself. No luck.
The river refused to swallow her drift. Then Pan,
who found this piece of washed-up flotsam, woke
Psyche to his sense of fair play — why let Eros
get off so easily as that? Spoiled brat,
Pan could not hunt or carry a tune, much less
make love — damn his aimless irresolute remote
control!

So Pan played against the gravity
of Psyche's case, to arouse her sense of being
a necessary, if not happy, part
of something else — a pattern, lesson, story —

in counterpoint. She had, so should have, nothing
to lose; then why not give this . . . her whole broken heart?

2. PANIC REVENGE, ON A FALSE NOTE

Not knowing where Eros had gone, Psyche searched out
her midwife-sisters, and as falsely played up to them
as they to her: to the tune of Eros, in light
of her abandonment, how he'd been overcome

with love for them; how if they would go to the same
high crag where Psyche'd been offered in sacrifice,
he'd meet them there. She lied, and they wanted him
so much, they believed. How easy, to reverse, revise
the score, rough draft after draft, rage-wrecked, tossed off.
Does love do the trick, or hate? Psyche's sisters fell for
a note they heard as tonic, true and leading up

to climax, kidnap, silence. Cliff-blind, tone-deaf
to rising panic, against the wind, the fools . . .
                                        That hope
craves murder, Psyche knew. And left that baggage behind her.

3. AT A LOSS

Quite hopeless in worldly terms, too sad
to feel sorry, too lost to bother to ask
the way, Psyche wandered, wondered how she could
compose herself, bring herself to the task
of settling other scores, Olympic ones,
of making trials. If only she had a sponsor.

She came to a courtyard heaped with seeds, grains,
sheaves gathered, scattered but promising some kind
of comfort. Could Demeter bear to take in one more
lost daughter? The goddess was sorry, but one double bind
was more than . . . (Aphrodite had been there beside
herself, besides . . .) Hera laughed. And Artemis quailed.
Hestia was cold, and even Athena paled.

Psyche's heart worn inside out turned out in spite
of all that brought her round to where Eros hid,
quivering in his mother's bed, live Psyche-bait.

4. APHRODITE'S PLACE

Psyche knew her future mother-in-law
would hardly throw a party for a mortal daughter.

How dare her son embarrass her like this; and how
dare this upstart mortal come beg favor?

Let Psyche visit her so-called husband: Him
on his sickbed thanks to her, his shoulder
so burned he can barely move. The utter shame
of his humiliation, to boot.
                              — Mother,
he'd said, she had a knife, she would have killed
me . . . but, she got a peek at what I am.
                                        (He smiled.)
— She thought I might be a snake. (He chuckled.)
Aphrodite kept a straight face. Left Eros's room.

5. MIXED-UP SEEDS

One handmaid, Habit, dragged Psyche by the hair
into Aphrodite's hall. Two others, Sorrow
and Trouble, pleased to obey their mistress's order,
whipped Psyche nearly blind. — I don't see how,
the goddess said, my son could love this creature,

except as a kitchen drudge. Psyche, you will show
how useful you are, in your way. There, on the floor,
you see a jumble of seeds, a mixed-up farrago —
wild oats, beans, millet, poppy, corn, chickpeas —
I don't like mixups. To start, you sort them out.

Psyche, sick and tired, could not have cared less.
She sat, a stupified lump. Around her feet,
a nervous swarm of ants began, on their own,
to sort, sift, order . . . Presto! — her task was done.

6. SEIZING THE SUN BY ITS HAIR

The goddess shrugs. A purely mechanical
dexterity hardly proves one's end divine.
As trials go, matching seeds is trivial.
And Psyche still thinks, obviously, her own

poor seed engrossing to Eros's. So Aphrodite
set her this next: go gather the golden wool
Apollo's wild rams hold so close. Our Psyche
goes out to sit by a stream. She's suicidal,

as usual. Barely notes Pan there fooling around
with Echo. Then, all at once, her vegetable cast
of mind turns fluid. A reed is giving her sound
advice:
           — When these rams go to sleep off their heat, you must —
quick — pluck the gold fluff snagged in twigs that comb
the beasts as they rut and stumble and graze.
                             Psyche comes
thus to gather, her wits whisked home
                         by cadence and lazy stream.

Her third task to do or undo is set before her:
to fill Aphrodite's favorite crystal vial
with water from the stream that splurges up
from Hell and loops back down to gorge Cocytus.

This time an eagle offers to help her call
Aphrodite's bluff by winging her up to a twist of rock
where the hell-bent water cramps and slows enough
to dip in and out without getting carried away.

She hardly cares to break into that cold
compulsive machine, an energy so self-
contained, pointless. Would it make sense someday?
Maybe to a child. Psyche does as she is told.
Her child? Her story's evidence? The child is pointing,
tugging — What's in that baby jug? A plaything?

8. SHOW AND TELL

How describe, looking back, this moment, her life?
A "miracle"? "challenge"? "a pretty fix"?
"hanging by a thread"? "a power dive"?
Will Psyche brag how she stole this trophy from the Styx?

Explain the ant farm and golden hairnet shelved
below? Who might her child prefer her mother to
be? — heroine or victim, ambitious or selved
by freak luck? Are these random curios, a few

of Grandma's old trinkets? How much of Psyche's tale
might a child want to know, believe, or need to bear?
Is there a lesson here? Nice, impersonal. . . .

A drop of "perpetual motion," as arrested here
from a mindless rush, transcends its original
conscription. . . .
                    The puzzled face will want better . . .

A better story.
                    — *So tell me if water can babble*
can water learn to think?
                    Psyche hears the child
in question wanting to take her shape from the tear-
drop curio, her place in transparency
and time.
          — *So tell me if the water is still wild*
when running is only reflecting once in a while?

What lasts is nothing if not invisible,
so Psyche thinks and thanks herself for being
transparent to her child as her child to her

will be.
          — *So let me tell you,*
                              her imaginary
child goes,
                    — *If I had found this prize instead of you,*
I would put something more to see inside.
OK?
          How very barely conceived this scene
. . . a seed, a fish, a pearl . . . ?
                              It was enough for Psyche to go on.

Canonic Etudes

I. A BEAUTY QUEEN'S LAST RESORT

Aprhodite is surprised, diverted, but mostly
annoyed by this mortal tart's appalling knack
for bold flunky luck. The goddess ups her ante.
Psyche's last (for surely this time she won't come back)

errand: to go to Hell. To mooch from Hades'
pale peerless queen a tiny casket full of her
rare top-grade night cream. Aphrodite,
so long in the spotlight, feels uglier than ever.

So Psyche sets off, with nothing but herself
to lose, and again the landscape's animal aura
talks her through: Hell's gates, the path to the river Styx;
an owl provides coins for the ferryman, a sylph
three cakes for Cerebus's three loud mouths, a cicada
the caution: to taste no food nor open any box.

2. THE POINT OF THE GAME

This time no ant's mechanics, no thoughtful reed,
no eagle will, like a stage-mother, organize
a ghost performance, hand Psyche title and deed.

That nature is behind her, she realizes,
and even *too far* behind. What lies ahead
depends on her own wits: to memorize
the tower's strategems, pose a charade
of duty, making sense. But Psyche's wise
at last to games well-won by seeing through
to core absurdities: To win, play as though

the game could matter, *as if* it could . . . to play
as if her life depends on the game, and not
vice versa . . . to play her hand of utter woe
as if . . . her nothing could be bothered to be

born. When, of course, this — *nothing* — is her only.

Thus Psyche sets out again, to sink as far
beneath herself as wink-and-grovel under mock-
maternal gazings, Hades' queen's, to be specific.
To melt one iced heart down to its puddling cure-
all dark cosmetic — an accidental kindness.

Funny, how even the Queen of Death, whose beauty,
as everyone knows, is invisible at best,
does sit-ups, courts dressings to kill, slathers cheek and thigh
"in-the-dark," plus calisthenics . . . Psyche wished
she knew, once upon a time, what she had to lose.

And does now. Or might. Oh yes. The child. She'd save
Aphrodite's wrinkled face in that case. Eros
could scarcely enter her mind at this point. To live
is ever moot, in questioning Psyche's alternative.

Fuga Inferni: *Psyche's* Opus Contra Naturam

I. GETTING THE GOODS

Persephone vowed how she always did admire
(if not adore) the celebrated mother
of Cupid. She agreed how all that sunlight's bad
for any body's complexion. She congratulated
the pregnant Psyche, and Aphrodite, the happy
grandmother-to-be. And she saw the compact filled,
with her special oil, her compliments. She told
its bearer not to mess with it. For Psyche to apply
such potent stuff to herself might harm the child
still womb-bound. A nightshade glint in Persephone's eye —

struck a nerve in Psyche. Queens could lie
beneath even mortal contempt. Why believe a gift
good for Aphrodite would be the death of Psyche?

2. EXTREME UNCTION

Her shadow, behind her like a pushy mother,
casts Psyche at last into Eros's more visible light,
her body solid. Her guilt and duty prod her,
in glimmers, toward pride, though she knows pride is the bane

of would-be heroes. Prod question: what's been done
toward undoing her . . . dumb thrall?
                                    And why deliver
to Aphrodite the fruits of lone Psyche's labor?
Having come this far, she's tempted to lift a lid.

To peek inside, at a masque her elder betters'
desire forbids her mortal hand and forehead
to touch? Her beauty by now must bear all their scars'

old battles perfected. Why not? Pry open, let light
air balm the covert, cure the mutual putrid
wound of rape addressed celestial, in Hell too . . . late.

3. FORMAL CHEMISTRY

Without her nerve, where would Psyche be? Without
the formal chemistry that conjugates
inertia into impulse, the boot that puts
its wheel of stellar spurs into the hot

flank of a matter and masters it? Her nerve
out-butterflies the weakest of belongings
to brute and elegant nature. Ours, ourselves
belonging only, but only, among other things

to stories. What is deeper than the frail
superficial laced with adamantine yet
invisible gall? Don't answer. The act is all
we ask, not knowing. Psyche delivers what

she promised on her way to being laid
aside, and nothing less than. . . .

                              You decide.

Psyche's Prelude Revised

1. A QUEEN'S CONFESSION

The midwife helped me feign to carry my "Psyche"
to term. When I lost this dot, she helped me mock
the emblem swoons, cravings: strapped on my pillow belly,
advised my labor's spell. From first faked stain
to afterbirth's bloody basin of aftermath, she rigged me fresh
from under her magic cloak in the wake of a cry.

"Keep mum about this diddle," Slyboots whispers,
"and your daughter will not die like mortal beauties."

Thrilled, I never questioned the use, care, curse,
or costs of my infant's immortality.
I wonder now, if I'd nixed the deal in time,
would I have a mortal daughter now to comfort,
tease, and let my future be? The shame
left behind by perfection is bound to hurt.

2. A KING'S CONFUSION

I let my wife keep her secret, not to admit
to losing a child of our loins. I duly fathered
a trick, this sprite, our illusion, the feather pillow
advancing toward labor, theatrically delivered.

I welcomed the child and spied the happy likeness
between our features and hers. I hired an artist
to touch up old family portraits, Psyche's nose
and eyes, chin, eyebrows and lips aptly forecast.

For a child of my flesh, I doubt I would have gone
to Delphi to assuage such beauty in extremity.
I would have scarred her a little, beaten her down
to human prospects, spoiled her enough to marry

an ordinary guy. As it was, I was as loath
as any suitor to touch her, and betrayed us both.

3. THE REAL MOTHER OF PSYCHE'S BEAUTY

I'm your typical midwife-witch, gorgeous and tough
as warty old stumps, sly milky eyes, my voice
a burdock's rasp on silk, hook-nosed, humped enough
in back to seem concave out front in my baby's

last month. If you think I'm going to tell you where
I picked up a seed to crash the egg I made
for Psyche, her *rara avis* yolk laced with more
magics than laid in wait for Leda's brood-mood,

forget it. I'm not that type. But go ahead
and speculate: foul play with an empty queen
is not beyond my pale. I meant for Cupid
to screw up with my daughter, but of course
not all their trouble could make either one the worse
for wear. Nor me, and most of the trouble was mine.

4. BOXING THE COMPASS

Sure, I'm talking Comedy, Dante no more nor less
than Genesis — the parts where language fails
to hold a scheme together . . . where maniac ego reels
from her potential, flops. A Paradiso's
inferior tensions at least keep up a show —
with egg-and-dart friezes, marble scrolls and such
elements as gravity lets be — the light touch
of spectral lines from stars kept distant. Who

can hope to box a compass without a fall
from grace, expected by the nature of
the spectacle, of those who watch for love
and dare's rude culmination? All downhill

from here. Not funny. But comic. I have to say,
Psyche would name her unborn burden Joy.

$\mathcal{N}$OTES

$\mathcal{A}$ Partial Glossary for "Box-Car Bertha"

black snake: a train carrying coal
boneyard: repair tracks
bo park: hobo camp
bundle stiff: a tramp
candy train: a train carrying jewels
count ties: walk on tracks
dangler: a freight train
fox: a hobo who manages to get inside passenger trains
gandy-dancer: a railroad section laborer, pick and shovel type
garden: railroad yard
glory: a train carrying nothing, empty box cars
grease the tracks: die
headender: head-on collision of trains
hotshot: a fast train
lettuce: money, greenbacks
moll-buzzers, cold hands, hoisters, door-matters, grifters, skin glommers: theives
of various kinds
pay station: a social welfare institution
pie-card mission: a mission that issues free meal tickets
plush-run: passenger train
prossy: prostitute
pull ear: talk
push daisies: be dead
rat stand: railroad depot
roofer: a hobo who rides the roofs of trains
secret works: brakes
shimmy-de-fer: railroad
short line: death
steel: tracks
"they": a social worker
varnish: a passenger train
X, crate, brownie, house car, box: a box car
Wabash Cannonball: a mythical, very fast train
whiffletree: coupling mechanism
whiz: aid brakes
worm drag: a train carrying silk

One Designing Women: Coco Chanel

III   Valette is an imaginary place in Chanel's childhood, a convent to which she said she and her sister were sent for the holidays. She often mentioned it. Aubazine, never mentioned by her, is probably the orphanage (also a convent) where she was taken by her father when her mother died. Of course, she had no real home to get home to.

VI   Jersey, the material Chanel surprisingly made fashionable, originally was developed for men's underwear in England, and until the advent of Chanel nobody seemed to want to buy it for anything. Her designs were revolutionary because they could be copied easily, made of inexpensive materials, and accompanied by costume jewelry without shame.

XI   The staircase referred to is that at the Rue Cambon where Chanel worked and where her fashions were shown and sold. She also received friends there.

XII   Chanel's tyrannical working habits are legendary. She designed her clothes primarily while her models were wearing them and walking back and forth between mirrors. She worked this group of young women mercilessly with threats and taunts, making them cry, ripping the dresses off them and pinning them back on, not always careful to avoid puncturing flesh with her pins.

    Chanel used to make her nose bleed on purpose (so she told someone, anyway) to get attention when she was a child.

All Isadora

    Isadora Duncan was born in 1878 and grew up in Oakland, California, in the same neighborhood as her close contemporary Gertrude Stein. She invented for herself a mode of interpretive dance—influenced first by the sea and later by her love of Greek art—that became the precursor of almost all forms of modern dance. Finding America paradoxically inimical to her innovations, she took her family to Europe, where she rapidly became famous—for her beauty, the novelty and passion of her dancing, her bare feet and filmy tunics, and her defense of free love.

    Isadora's passion for the dance was matched only by her passion for children and for the establishment of a school where every aspect of her students' lives would be guided by her concepts of freedom for both body and mind. Her schools, first in Grünewald, Germany, then in Paris, and finally in Russia, were all constantly beset by financial difficulties, even though she poured most of her own earnings into them and made pleas for help, giving concerts with her troupe of "Isadorables" wherever and whenever she could.

    The great tragedy of Isadora's life was the death of her own two children, Deirdre (whose father was Gordon Craig) and Patrick (whose father was the sewing machine heir, Paris Singer), by drowning in 1913. After a period of inconsolable grief, she returned to dancing and the establishment of her school. Still failing to find backing in Europe or America, she departed for Russia in 1921, with a promise of aid from the Bolsheviks. The aid did not materialize. Disillusioned, she returned to Paris, this time accompanied by the young Russian poet Sergei Esenin. She had married Esenin to facilitate his leaving Russia, and she was devoted to him, although he caused her much pain and precipitated the failure of her last attempt to tour America. After this, her career floundered.

The story of Isadora's death is well known. As she was about to go for a test drive in a sports car she was interested in buying (and could in no way afford), her long scarf became entangled in the spoke of the rear wheel. When the car started to move, she was instantly strangled. At this time, September 1927, she had nearly completed her commissioned autobiography, *My Life* (New York: Horace Liveright, Inc., 1927), in which she wrote, "My life has known but two motives—Love and Art—and often Love destroyed Art, and often the imperious call of Art put a tragic end to Love. For these two have no accord, but only constant battle."

The Terrible Memory of Lizzie Borden

Every American schoolchild knows the rhyme:

> Lizzie Borden took an ax,
> Gave her mother forty whacks.
> When she saw what she had done,
> She gave her father forty-one.

Actually, Lizzie's stepmother's skull was found, upon autopsy, to have about nineteen ax wounds, her father's only ten. The date was August 4, 1892.

Lizzie and the Bordens' maid Maggie were the only persons present in or around the house at the time of the murders, Lizzie's sister Emma (ten years older) being out of town and Mr. Borden's brother-in-law (Lizzie's mother's brother) John, who was an overnight guest, having departed early on the morning of the crime. The police in Fall River, where the Borden family had long been well established, performed a sloppy initial investigation, and on August 11, 1892, arrested Lizzie based on circumstantial evidence. The notorious trial, in June of 1893, resulted in Lizzie's acquittal by a jury of men who could not bring themselves to believe, despite considerable evidence, that such brutality could come from a well-brought-up daughter who had been a Sunday school teacher and a member of the Hospital Board, the WCTU, and the Fruit and Flower Mission. Since then, thousands of pages have been written in elaboration and further investigation of the Fall River decision.

Lizzie Andrew Borden was born in 1860. Her mother died in 1862, leaving her and twelve-year-old Emma. In 1865 Mr. Borden married Abby, who was five feet tall and weighed, at the time of her death, about two hundred pounds. Lizzie was never very fond of her, and was less fond as time went on. Mr. Borden was an undertaker who had the reputation of cutting off the feet of his clients to fit them into cheaper caskets. He left this lucrative business to make still more money in real estate, yet he remained one of the most miserly men in town. Lizzie resented his insane stinginess but loved him nonetheless. In 1891, possibly during one of her "spells" (a form of ambulatory epilepsy followed by amnesia?), Lizzie broke into her stepmother's dressing room and stole money and jewelry. Her father, realizing, covered for her and henceforth left the key to that room in view as a reminder. But he was not always so kind. In May 1892 he slaughtered with an ax all of the pigeons Lizzie had been devotedly keeping as pets. A few months later, the Bordens were found murdered in the same way.

Lizzie could never get her alibis straight. She had a terrible memory. But she had luck. After her acquittal she moved to a fashionable part of town, changed her name to Lizbeth, drove her sister away, and gave disreputable parties (by Fall River standards) for Boston theater people. She willed most of her money to the Animal Rescue League.

The Passions of Rahel Varnhagen

RAHEL LEVIN VARNHAGEN VON ENSE (1771–1833)

What a history!—A fugitive from Egypt and Palestine, here I am and find help, love, fostering in you people. With real rapture I think of these origins of mine and this whole nexus of destiny, through which the oldest memories of the human race stand side by side with the latest developments. The greatest distances in time and space are bridged. The thing which all my life seemed to me the greatest shame, which was the misery and misfortune of my life—having been born a Jewess—this I should on no account now wish to have missed.

— Words said on her deathbed by Rahel (Antonie Friederike Robert) Varnhagen von Ense, as reported by her husband, Karl August Varnhagen von Ense

The woman does not actually judge; she has the subject, and insofar as she does not possess it, it does not concern her.

— Goethe, referring to Rahel's comments on his work, in published excerpts from her correspondence with Varnhagen

No philanthropic list, no cheers, no condescension, no mixed society, no new hymn book, no bourgeois star, nothing, nothing could ever placate me. . . . You will say this gloriously, elegiacally, fantastically, incisively, extremely jestingly, always musically, provokingly, often charmingly; you will say it all very soon. But as you do, the text from my old, offended heart will still have to remain yours.

— Rahel Levin

CHRONOLOGY OF THE LIFE OF RAHEL VARNHAGEN

1771, May 19	Rahel born in Berlin, eldest child of well-to-do merchant Markus Levin. The family is Orthodox, speaks Yiddish.
c. 1790	Father's death.
1794	Rahel visits relatives in Breslau, is appalled.
c. 1790–1806	Rahel's salon in an attic room on Jägerstrasse to which almost all the important intellectuals of Berlin come: the Humboldt brothers, Friedrich Schlegel, Friedrich Gentz, Friedrich Schleier-

macher, Prince Louis Ferdinand of Prussia and his mistress, Friedrich August Wolf, Jean Paul, Brentano, Ludwig Tieck, Adelbert von Chamisso, etc.

1795–96, winter	Rahel meets Count Karl von Finckenstein. Engagement protracted until 1800.
c. 1800	Rahel's brother Ludwig baptized. He assumes the name Robert.
1801	Rahel meets Friedrich Gentz.
1801–2	She meets the secretary of the Spanish Legation, Don Raphael d'Urquijo, and is engaged to him.
1804	Break with Urquijo.
1806, October 27	Napoleon enters Berlin. The war causes Rahel's circle of friends to break up. Soon after the wealth of the Levin family is reduced.
1808, spring	Rahel begins relationship with Karl August Varnhagen.
1809, spring	Rahel meets Alexander von der Marwitz.
1809–11	Varnhagen rises in the military as an accomplished attaché.
1810	Rahel starts calling herself Rahel Robert.
1811	Varnhagen takes Rahel from Berlin to Teplitz.
1814, summer	After travels, publications of correspondence between Rahel and Varnhagen concerning Goethe, more travels due to war, and severe illness, Rahel gets together with Varnhagen again at Teplitz.
1814, September	Rahel returns to Berlin, is baptized, and is married to Varnhagen. She takes the name Antonie Friederike.
1815, September 8	Goethe calls on Rahel in Frankfurt.
1821–32	Berlin salon of the Varnhagens. Prominent visitors: Bettina von Arnim, Heine, Prince Bückler-Muskau, Hegel, Ranke, Eduard Gans.
1833, March 7	Rahel dies.

Simone Weil: Hunger's Fool

It is impossible, in a brief section of notes, to indicate all that links my poems to the life and writings of Simone Weil, all that is left out or assigned to a position between the lines. I have chosen to emphasize the hunger and the food of her thought, as literally as is metaphorically possible. This is only one of a number of possible approaches to her astonishing life, and I hope it is not too reductive.

Most of the aphoristic statements in the poems may be found, more or less succinctly, in the notebooks of Simone Weil: *First and Last Notebooks* (New York: Oxford University Press, 1970), and *The Notebooks of Simone Weil,* 2 vols. (New York: G. P. Putnam's Sons, 1956).

For biographical information I consulted the following: *Simone Weil: A Sketch for a Portrait,* by Richard Rees (Carbondale: Southern Illinois University Press, 1966), and *Simone Weil: A Fellowship in Love,* by Jacques Cabaud (New York: Channel Press, 1964).

I DIALOGUE: During World War I, beginning when Simone was five, both she and her brother André sent their sugar rations to soldiers at the front. At ten, despite her fierce patriotism, Simone was outraged by the way France humiliated her former enemy. Yet even at that age, she insisted on humiliating her own body. She washed in cold water although her health was delicate, and she forced herself to perform strenuous physical tasks despite her clumsiness. Though André was older, she competed with him in reciting Racine from memory, agreeing that the one who "dried up" first would be slapped by the other. The migraines that tortured her throughout her life began at twelve. Her response was to try to seek truth through pain, to *use* suffering. Thus the pattern of her entire life was established in early childhood.

II PROVIDENCE: "Any plan that can be discerned in events, whatever it may be, is one of Providence's plans—among an infinity of others" (*First and Last Notebooks,* p. 72).

As a student, Simone was remarkable because of her physical awkwardness, her passion for tobacco (she rolled her own cigarettes—messily), clothes that seemed chosen for their lack of fit, and her idiosyncratic pronunciation of French, giving her native language a slight foreign accent.

Simone's first published essay concerned the image of Proteus, and she often returned to it.

"Twelve o'clock: it's time for lunch"—this became, for Simone and her fellow students at the Ecole Normale, a catchword repeated whenever one couldn't find an answer to a disconcerting question. It began when Simone asked such a question of Professor Bouglé (director of school studies and personal bête noire of hers) in class, and he responded with this ploy.

III BITTER-SWEET: After leaving school, Simone was involved simultaneously in teaching philosophy at a middle-class girls' school and fighting for the rights of workers. Her valiant attempt to reconcile class struggles on both fronts with her own idealism was appreciated neither by her own employers nor by those of the workers.

1934: Simone obtained leave from her teaching job at Roanne and found a job in the Alsthom electrical works of Paris. She wanted firsthand experience of manual labor. She operated a furnace shutter—heavy work at which she was not by any means competent.

IV JUSTICE: "All life is reading." "Reading" is, for Simone Weil, a technical term for the process by which the mind interprets what the eye sees.

V DENIAL: Simone Weil, following Plato, often referred to society, or any collectivity within it, as a form of "the Great Beast."

Simone, her awkwardness as a soldier not unnoticed, was left behind on the Aragon front to cook for the Anarchist troops she had joined. She was, however, no better at cooking than she was at handling a gun. She spilled boiling oil on herself in her first efforts and was taken to a hospital from which her parents rescued her, bringing her home to France. The Spanish Civil War left her badly disillusioned as well as seriously wounded.

VI FAITH: In 1937 Simone traveled in Italy. Aesthetic contemplation fed her spiritual contemplation and somewhat altered the thrust of her political thought, though she never lost sight of her ultimate aims for improving the lives of the working classes; nor did she change her notions about the spiritual value of physical labor.

From the notebooks: "Eve began it. If humanity was lost because she ate a fruit, then . . . looking at a fruit without eating it should be what saves humanity."

VII REDEMPTION: This poem recounts a mystical vision Simone experienced in connection with her frequent repetition to herself of Herbert's poem "Love," her favorite. Her own account may be found on the last pages of *The Notebooks of Simone Weil,* vol. 2. It was a turning point; it intensified her involvement with Christianity but did not lead her to conversion.

VIII THE BUNCH OF GRAPES: During the Occupation, Simone was suspended from teaching because of her Jewish origins. She protested eloquently to the Vichy government in a letter in which she also thanked its officials for giving her two precious gifts they themselves did not possess: respect for the earth and poverty. Her letter was never answered.

In the fall of 1941, Simone spent some time harvesting grapes in Saint-Marcel d'Ardèche and teaching Greek to Father Gustave Thibon, with whose family she stayed. During this time she constantly repeated the Lord's Prayer in Greek as a form of meditation while she worked. In her translation of the prayer, "daily" bread appears as "supernatural" bread, a change she was free to make, as the Greek word is a hapax legomenon.

Amare amabam: I love the act of loving itself. This was prescribed by Simone as an ideal, as well as a cure for that state wherein love has no other object.

IX   DISCIPLINE: Simone agonized at not being able to take an active part in the resistance in occupied France. She did not want to leave Europe with her parents, who were urging her to accompany them to New York, but at last it seemed the only way she might have of eventually getting to London to join the Free French there.

Simone fervently hoped to be assigned some mission, preferably dangerous, to help her country. She became obsessed with plans for a women's nursing corps that would bring plasma and first aid directly to the front lines— essentially a suicide corps. The plan was rejected by the French government from the start and later by the English and American governments as well.

Simone sailed to New York on the *Serpa Pinto* in the summer of 1942.

X   THE COLLAR: In the fall of 1912, Simone finally obtained passage to London. One Catholic friend was concerned that she was undertaking a dangerous crossing without having been baptized first. Wanting neither to insult her friend nor to convert, Simone replied that she thought the Atlantic Ocean would be a fine baptistry.

The connection between war and dreams is made clear in Simone Weil's unfinished play *Venice Restored,* one line of which states that "weapons make dreams more potent than reality" (act 2, sc. 6). Meanwhile, Simone was trying to convince the Free French that her ill health was an asset in espionage— namely, she would die with the smallest amount of torture.

XI   AFFLICTION: When Simone was spending holidays from school with her aunt in the country, she liked to fill her time by digging potatoes ten hours a day. While in college, she spent two summers visiting her mother's friend Pierre Le Tellier at St. Malo de Lalande near Coutances in Normandy. Here she worked furiously at harvest time and would (to the horror of the regular reapers) gather up in her bare arms the thistles that were meant to be picked up by men with pitchforks.

In 1941, when Simone was picking grapes at Saint-Marcel d'Ardèche, her employer gave her what was the highest possible compliment: that she was fit to be a peasant's wife.

XII   AFFLICTION STILL: The concluding sentence of Simone Weil's essay on the adventure of Proteus: "Geometry, like all thought, perhaps, is the daughter of labor's fortitude."

XIII   LOVE: The epigraph to this last sonnet is from Simone's favorite poem, connected with her vision of 1938 (see VII and its note).

Simone Weil's last letter to her parents speaks of the dessert the English call a "fool" and compares it (unfavorably) to Shakespeare's fools.

Death certificate: "Cardiac failure due to myocardial degeneration of the heart muscles due to starvation and pulmonary tuberculosis. The deceased did kill and slay herself by refusing to eat whilst the balance of her mind was disturbed."

ADN-5964   8/13/98